I0192518

loop

B. 10

peek-Kasteel

th Africa

795 2701

werh@yahoo.com

The Real Yahoo.

By Hendrik Bruwer

The Real Yahoo.

By Hendrik Bruwer

PART ONE

Chapter One

23 MARCH

FRIDAY MORNING

Listen, I don't want to sound like Forrest Gump or Tom Sawyer by telling you of how lucky I was to have had an exciting life by going on and on about my days as a ping-pong player and of how I went on a treasure hunt with my old friend Huck. I really don't want to sound anything like that, especially not on my birthday of all days and… and I also don't want you to see it as your duty in reading all of this as it is your duty to read the Bible or some other boring book that you don't like reading because then there's no point for me telling you all this. All… all I'm going to do is that I'm going to tell you a few things here and there about myself because today is my birthday and I don't feel like sharing it with anyone in particular. My mother made me breakfast this morning and it was nice and I thanked her for it and everything, but I really don't feel like sharing my birthday today.

I don't know why you know, because it's my birthday and later on tonight I probably should go out partying and get drunk with people that keep on telling me that I'm a great guy living in a city with, you know… great potential. But today… today is my birthday, my special day, and if I don't feel like wasting the little money I have to go out partying and getting drunk, well then that's special enough for me.

My mother, she went out for the day with her boyfriend who calls himself Michael K. She did invite me to come along, just because it being my birthday you know, but I don't feel like spending a birthday with those two either. Both of them are lunatics.

So I lied to my mother when I said I was going out with a few friends of mine. Actually, what I plan to do and I'm not kidding, is to stay here in my room all day telling you a little bit of what went wrong in my life.

Yes it sounds depressing, especially on a birthday, but don't worry, I'm not going to commit suicide when I'm finished doing it.

Trust me, I'm not that crazy.

I'm not a suicidal character at all.

And don't start worrying if you think that I'm not that

a great company. I promise I'm not going to bore you to death. I don't think it's the kind of story that'll bore. Like I said it's not the Bible. Okay, so it won't change your life, I admit that, but… but that's not the point.

The point is that I once shook hands with the President. I really did. Had a chat with him and everything. One of the greatest moments of my life that one. And don't you think that is worth telling, eh?

I'll tell you some other stuff too, trust me and hopefully you'll catch on my whole philosophy on life also and maybe you'll understand why a good-looking guy like me who holds a crappy job, spends a birthday in his room all by himself. Maybe you'll figure it all out.

Anyway, my name is Alvy… Alvy CLEMENS and just between you and me I'm twenty-one years old today and I'm very good-looking I really am. I look like a movie star I promise. I tell you it's hard to put my good looks into any form of meaningful or coherent sentence; that's how good-looking I am. I even starred in this TV commercial once, some crappy cereal ad, but I really don't think it's such a big deal, except for my mother. Poor thing. She still thinks that I'm well on my way towards fame and fortune.

But I have a great personality also. A real charmer

they say. My mother always says I talk too fast and that

maybe I should work on that as a social skill of some

sorts, but I figure she's just jealous because I really do

attract pretty girls because of my charming character.

I've got a Jewish nose, kind of pointy and everything, but

believe me when I say that around here few are perfect.

And yes, in case you're wondering I'm also a South African

trying to make a living here in Cape Town. I tell you,

it's not that easy.

Chapter Two

I can't really say how it all came about, but I remember

when I was still a kid and how my mother kept on asking me
silly questions of what I wanted to do with my life.
That, I think, is where the whole mess fell into place.

'So Alvy CLEMENS,' she would say. 'What do you want to
do with your life, eh?'

I tell you my mother asked me silly questions like that
nearly every damn day and it kind of freaked me out after
a while.

'Alvy CLEMENS! Tell your mother what you want to do
when you're a grown man!'

I also remember the time when I was still at school and
how the children at the playground always looked so silly
when they screamed in my face,

'Oh, I'm going to be a doctor!' or

'I'd like to be a firefighter!' or

'Ah, I'm going to be a preacher!'

Irritating things like that.

Those children were so young; half of them were
probably still wetting their pants, but believe me they
already knew what they wanted to do when they were all big
and strong. It sounded to me that what I was going to do
when I'm all big and strong was the most important thing
that there is, more important than just enjoying myself
and enjoying myself was the only thing I really cared

about when I was still a kid. To me it made no sense, no
sense at all, this you're big and strong business.

See… I wasn't like any of them. I couldn't just say
that I wanted to be this or that when I'm all big and
strong. It made no damn logical sense. So all I kept
telling the little children at the playground was that, 'I
just want to be… you know, famous, that's all,' and that's
why when I see a famous person I like I say I want to be
like him. Like in sports, everyone wants to be like Tiger
Woods or David Beckham, you know, somebody famous.

That's the kind of kid who I was.

I admit that one has to have lots of luck to become
world famous like those two. It is kind of like winning
the national lottery or playing poker, becoming famous and
all, except if you're not cut out to be famous. What I
mean by that is that some people just don't have it in
them to become famous.

I know people get so personal about how they look and
all, but for me particularly, girls must have a really
tough time of it when they want to be a famous actress
when they're not actually pretty. I feel sorry for them
to be honest.

I don't want to run those girls down by crushing all
their dreams and aspirations.

But, I do think that if you want to avoid a long depression and thoughts of suicide then you should stay away from becoming a famous actress.

Personally and I mean personally, I don't mind seeing girls that aren't so good-looking on TV at all, just as long as they can act a bit, but I tell you, most men don't give a damn about the acting sides of things. They just don't.

Some things will never change although nowadays, you girls can go to the plastic surgeon; do some liposuction, lift your breasts, make it bigger and all that crazy little things that I don't even want to think about right now. I can understand why girls do that sort of thing because it's very important how a person looks, especially with the whole feminist thing women have now got going. I still figure though that I'd rather have sex with an old fashion girl than with these pumped up sex machines you get nowadays.

I tell you, they're relentless.

Anyway, I had my fifteen minutes of being famous. Yup, there was this one time I remember when I was sixteen. Long time ago. I got picked to star in this TV commercial, because the producers thought I was kind of good-looking and everything.

It was this cereal ad, real corny if you want to know my personal opinion. You see, anyone could've starred in it because… because all I had to do was to eat cereal, like I was really enjoying it of course. I also had to make sure that the cereal milk dripped slowly out of my mouth, while I was eating the cereal of course, because the cereal was supposed to be really tasty. To tell you the truth, that cereal tasted like crap.

Anyway, this commercial, it was like kind of a musical, with ballerinas and prostitutes and while I was eating the damn bowl of cereal there were these extras, these awful theatre people with their dance routines, prancing around me like a bunch of lunatics as if the cereal was some kind of darn magic potion and… and all I kept doing was eating the crap cereal. As if it was really tasty.

Just terrific.

At the end I had to say a few irrelevant words to the camera, just… just for the sake of saying irrelevant words to the camera. And that was it you know. I don't even remember my line. But everybody loved the commercial, they really did and I still get people wanting to know whether I'm the good-looking guy who starred in 'that TV commercial.' It's somewhat embarrassing now you know when I have time to reflect on the whole chapter, but back then

I really thought of myself as someone famous and
important. I even got lured to make a name for myself in
the industry for naked people, for there was a lot of
money there to be made also and I was happy for all the
attention. It was an attractive offer and I thought long
and hard over it, but it's a pretty full-time thing though
and I didn't feel comfortable being naked all the time.

But… but to be honest here, I like actually being on
my own and stuff. Yeah, I'm quite an introverted
individual to tell you the truth. People can sometimes be
a bit overwhelming you know and when I'm famous… being
surrounded by lunatics all day long, signing junk
autographs and all that – it's not my idea of fun you
know. Not that I did sign autographs or anything back
then. But imagine Alvy CLEMENS goes out to fetch the
newspaper in the mornings or goes out to watch a movie
with a girl he fancies. Let's pretend for a minute that
I'm famous, very famous. Now… do you know what Alvy
CLEMENS does when he wakes up early in the morning,
besides of course the things we don't tell each other?

Well, to tell you the truth, most mornings I go and I
fetch the newspaper in my underwear at the street café
just around the corner from where I live here in Brooklyn,
Cape Town. It's a CLEMENS thing. Now… if I'm famous,

like really famous, I won't be able to do that sort of thing you see. Besides from being followed by some nutcase or lunatic all day, when I'll sit down to read the newspaper, the whole newspaper would be full of stories of me in my ugly underwear. They will discuss everything in detail, of what size my underwear was and what kind of underwear it was also. I love walking around in my underwear you know. It's… it's one of the best things a man can do and… and I really don't want to buy the newspaper to see what kind of underwear I was wearing and I really don't want to read about myself either. You see, that's the other side of being famous. To be honest, I don't give a damn about my own underwear because I don't even buy my own underwear. That's my mother's department. I tell you, my mother get her kicks from buying me cheap underwear.

Anyway, I was still telling you about my mother, of how she asked me again and again of what I wanted to do with my life. I, Alvy CLEMENS, little damn child who just wanted to have fun, came up with this:

'Mom, I think I want to get my face on TV and in newspapers and in magazines so that people will think of me as someone important. Like you know… somebody famous.'

My mother, she's not the cleverest of woman. Yes, she cooks nice meals and she keeps the house tidy and everything, but she doesn't really know what's going on in the world. I don't think she even knows who the current President is.

'Oh, so you want to be like a politician or somebody, like the President?'

'Like who?'

'The President.'

'Gee mom, don't know about you know, the President, but yeah… somebody like that. Somebody pretty important and flashy would do.'

'Oh, that sounds good, really interesting. Your father always said you were special in some way.'

'He did?'

'Of course. Your dad was very proud of you.'

'Thanks mom,' I said.

'You're not like everybody else, Alvy CLEMENS,' she said. 'You've got character.'

'What do you mean?'

'You're special.'

'But special in what?'

'You'll figure it out. Go and be famous Alvy. Yes, go and do that.'

'I can?'

'Oh, make me proud Alvy CLEMENS, make me proud!' she
always brayed like a damn donkey. Sometimes she still
does.

I tell you, I try hard with my mother I really do. But
after my dad died she really got depressed and everything
and nowadays she's just another crazy middle-aged woman
who gets her kicks in buying me cheap underwear whilst
speaking about what it is to have character.

You see, my mother got real depressed after my dad died
three years ago of the freaking cancer and she just hasn't
been the same since. She sees a psychiatrist now and
again who tells her that she's a manic-depressive and
borderline schizophrenic and she thinks she's very special
because of it. I'm not really into mental illness, but my
personal opinion is that she's making up all these fancy
diseases just so that everyone may feel sorry for her. If
anything she's a darn hypochondriac if you know what that
is.

My dad and I, well what can I say, we weren't that
close. What's funny, now that he's dead I don't even miss
him to tell you the truth. He was one of those silent
types; didn't talk much. I… I remember when we ate dinner
and my dad usually ate in silence not even registering

that my mom and I was busy with each other's throats at the other end of the table. Only when he had a couple of drinks in him, the son of the bitch would mutter a lousy few words. He was a bit of a head case, my dad. One of those thinker types.

I remember my dad always begged me to come along to the construction yard where he worked so that I could spend more quality time with him, but hell, construction wasn't something that really interested me. My dad probably figured that his son was going to keep the CLEMENS tradition going in the construction business, but things never got that far. To tell you the truth, I'm not really into hard labr.

But mother loved dad a lot and I think his silent character had a real calming influence on her. I guess they were compatible considering how my mother acts nowadays. I tell you she's a whining old gypsy grandmother. I swear; she keeps on repeating the same things over and over as if I'm deaf or something. What a bore. She again, talks way too much. What's worse, when she talks, everybody stops listening.

What I mean is: she talks rubbish.

But she has a boyfriend these days, an achievement in itself when you consider that she's gone mental. Michael

K. is the guy's name. Also not a rocket scientist if you know what I mean, but he… he helps around the house now and then when he thinks he's too much of a nuisance which in my opinion is almost all of the time. Also a bit of a head case, that Michael K. character.

You can actually say the two of them deserve each other, my mother and Michael K. that is, because… because there's definitely something wrong with both of them when it comes to using their brains properly. I tell you, I don't think any scientists should check out my mother and that Michael K.'s brains for any scientific clues because they'll find more questions than answers.

I don't know if those two have any plans or anything, like getting married or making a bunch of babies, but I really don't give a damn at this point in time. As long as I keep my room tidy and as long as I have a good and steady job, my dear mother, she'll still think that I'm the greatest thing that has ever happened to her even though she feels like stabbing me to death sometimes.

And that's another problem.

Another big problem.

I've never had a good and steady job so we always struggle with the money sides of things. I remember my mother once considering prostitution, but I figure she was

just pulling my leg. She's way too old for that and
prostitutes are supposed to be darn attractive anyhow.
Gee, my mother would've struggled with that profession.
Picturing her going down? It would've been a tough old
Christmas.

But yeah, my mother and I would've probably starved to
death a long time ago if it weren't for my uncle. My
Uncle Lennie, he and my two nephews, Ronnie and Joe, they
lived a few blocks away from us in this very same
neighborhood with Ronnie and Joe being his sons of course.
Uncle Lennie helped us a lot over the years he really did.

Chapter Three

Oh, I nearly forgot. It's called Brooklyn, our

neighborhood I mean. It's situated in the northern

suburbs of the city and one can actually see the whole of

Table Mountain from this side, the north side, or the best

part of it I should say. At night especially the mountain

looks quite pretty and surprisingly peaceful bearing in

mind that it's surrounded by millions of crazy people who

only want to tingle their genitals. Hey, it's the truth.

We're all part of the animal kingdom in this city.

Other than that though, Cape Town is just like any

other place, beautiful out of those tourist magazines, but

darn ugly when you're trying to make a living inside of

it.

Brooklyn especially. I don't think Mark Shuttleworth

or the President will ever consider buying property here

in this neighborhood if you know what I mean. It's too

much of a mess. Every street here got potholes. Don't

ask me why, but a pothole is a Brooklyn tourist attraction

and very infectious because our trees, they again suffer

from some kind of diarrhea. None of them show any colour

and all.

We have this library though and it again consists only

of Mark Twain books, but if you're into Mark Twain

literature don't worry that much because… because most of

us around here don't bother with literature. Nobody has

touched <u>The Adventures of Tom Sawyer</u> for years. Trust me I checked. There's an outdated magazine section and I guess that's where you'll find the reading population. We don't bother much with education. You know, my old high school? They don't have a principle. Yeah, the previous bastard was arrested for turning the place into a brothel and now there's no one to fill his position. I bet you that same bastard will get out of prison and he'll still be principal.

Every damn house here in Brooklyn looks exactly like the next one. Not very spectacular to say the least. Definitely not a tourist destination. Definitely not. Don't make a mistake; our house, the CLEMENS house that is, it looks perfectly normal under the circumstances. There are rooms in it and it has a kitchen also, but still, I don't think a world famous architect designed it. Who knows, maybe he did and it was his first attempt. I guess the only positive thing about this neighborhood is our damn liquor store because it has never gotten of business and I also hear it's expanding. We Brooklynites look up to that store.

About the TV commercial I starred in that I told you about

earlier. You probably want to know more and I can
understand why the curiosity and crap, but… but
personally, I don't know what the big fuss is. You see…
it was actually my mother's idea. She really had high
hopes of me becoming famous and everything after I told
her about it, and… and when her eyes came across an ad in
the newspaper that read pretty faces for a commercial, my
mother nearly had one of those epileptic seizures again.
Yeah, she suffers from that thing as well.

Anyway, next thing you know, Alvy CLEMENS became a big
shot in the TV commercial industry at the age of sixteen.

Yahoo.

The commercial I was in, I remember it ran on and off
for almost three years on television after that. It
became kind of a hit, like a bestseller. Everybody in my
neighborhood nearly had a heart attack when my commercial
was up and running that's how big it was. However, every
time I watched that ad on television I wanted to throw up,
that's how much I hated it. I still do and what's worse,
I still get demented characters confronting me whether I'm
that guy in the corny TV commercial with the bowl of
cereal.

My mother as you can expect was over the moon with it
all. You know, because of all the attention I was getting

being a television star and everything. She already saw
me as some famous actor. That's right. And I, I was only
sixteen years old, still an ignorant little kid who wanted
to have fun. Gee, to be in the limelight was tough
enough, but… but with all my fellow Brooklynites wishing
me all the best made it even tougher.

My dad, he was still alive back then but like I said,
the guy was a complete mute. He hardly spoke so I never
knew his opinion on the subject. Gee, I wish he would've.

Anyway, the producers of that TV commercial thought
along the same spectrum as my mother were thinking, that
I'm terrific because of my good looks and all. I was very
flattered and everything having all the attention and
stuff, but I personally never had much of an eye for
acting. I… I just don't like staring into cameras the
whole time and it makes me a bit self-conscious,
especially with this Jewish nose I got to deal with.

Actually, what I wanted to do is this:

I wanted to be a stockbroker. Honestly.

I watched this motion picture one time eh… this <u>Wall
Street</u> picture and I really loved it. You know that
Michael Douglas actor? Well, he played this billionaire
Gordon Gecko who made lots of money out of stocks, in the
picture of course. Now, I don't know if you've ever

watched that <u>Wall Street</u>. But if you didn't, then I'm

recommending it you to go and see it. It's pretty darn

good I tell you. One of my all time favourites.

You see… I wanted to be like that… yes, that Gordon

Gecko character, the stockbroker billionaire in the motion

picture who didn't give a damn about anyone except… except

about himself.

Just like me.

What I liked about him, besides from what I just said

and him having a lot of money of course, is that he also

had such a crazy outlook on life and you know, I kind of

liked it. Like for instance, when… when he had a

philosophy on money and stuff, he would say something in

the line of, 'Make lots of it and screw the rest.' Not

that he actually said it, but that's what I think he

meant.

Or on friendship he'll say, 'Go and get a dog sonny.

You can't trust a human being.' Not that he said it, but

that's what I think he meant.

Yes, the guy's crazy. A lunatic to be precise, but

personally I like people who are mental.

It makes them rather interesting.

So… so I wanted to be a stockbroker, right? Right. I

hope you're still attentive and all. I just gotten out of

school and it was about that time when my dad died of
cancer.

But don't worry, it wasn't a tragedy.

My dad was a silent type and we couldn't get through to
each other. There was no chemistry, nothing.

My mother was devastated though, especially because it
meant that she had to start working again.

Oh, my mother is a social worker. Yeah, I don't
believe it either but I also don't get it either; she gets
these crazy impulses to help people all of a sudden. I
mean what about me? I'm lonely like hell.

But I tell you, if I didn't talk some sense into her
back then with the social work and all, she would've done
it for free. That's how big a nutcase she is. Trust me,
she's not a prostitute. That was just a joke.

Anyway, for the sake of my mother, just for the sake of
the poor old lady, I featured in another couple of TV
commercials, but it was just to please my damn mother
because the money it was good. Also the fact that her
only child makes an appearance on television now and
again, it made my mother feel rather important in our
neighborhood. But… but like I said to you just now, I had
my hopes on becoming a famous and successful stockbroker
by then. That was my thing.

Chapter Four

I'll skip the part of where I eventually broke my mother's
spirits in me sharing my plans to be a successful
stockbroker. Believe me you don't want to hear it. It's
way too long and depressing and besides, you probably
forgot that it's my birthday, eh? I'm not going to
depress myself even more by talking about my mother on my
damn birthday of all days.

   She needs help.

But… but regarding this stockbroking business, I liked it
even when I was little. I really did you know. I
remember… I remember how I picked a stock in the daily
newspaper that we had, and how I followed it for a few
days and every day I remember, I would take out my
calculator to see how much money I've gained or lost from
that same stock. Yeah, it was fun. I didn't play stocks
in real life you know. My dad, he did when he was still
alive. I helped him a little in that.

   But boy, I don't think my genius of a dad was as
interested in stocks as I was. Sometimes he just didn't
even bother to check his stocks. Just didn't bother.

   Anyway, my mother couldn't afford to pay for the

university tuition. Naturally I had to take out a big
loan from the bank with my Uncle Lennie as the sponsor and
all. You know what? I still owe a fair share of the loan
to the bank, but I really try not to think about it
because it's a scary thought. It really is and I don't
want to get thrown in prison or anything for something
that wasn't even my fault.

Oh, something else. Hmm… I was in prison before. I
know, it's not something I should feel proud about. I'm
actually kind an embarrassed by it. But… but it's not as
if I robbed a bank or something like that. I also didn't
make the front pages or anything. And I don't belong to a
terrorist organization if that's what you're thinking.

I'm a good person, I promise. I just got into trouble
this one time where I stole a box of chocolates out of a
supermarket store. No big deal. Oh then… then there was
this one time where I stole this nice shirt out of a
clothing store. The funny thing is, I didn't even felt
the need for a shirt that time.

I'm a kleptomaniac I swear.

Oh, and then there was also this one… eh… never mind.
You get the picture.

Hmm… wasn't I telling you about my days as a student,
eh?

Well, once upon a time I was a student.   A lousy one
of course.

Let me see… the university.   It was okay I guess.
Especially in the beginning where one didn't necessarily
felt obligated to go to classes and everything.   Now that
was the best.   Just great.   I also made some great friends
who too fancied being stockbrokers.   There was like a
common interest if you know what I mean.   That was good
also.   And the girls… they were real pretty.   Very decent
too and I remember that it took me five dates to get into
bed with this one girl who sat next to me in class.   Yeah,
five dates.   Now that's what I call plain decency.   You
see, here in Brooklyn, us Brooklynites?   We don't go for
dates that much.   I'm serious.

Here it's just business.

I tell you, the university opened my eyes for the very
first time.   Just all the culture and sophistication
around there, all the intellectuals, all the decency.
It's hard to describe.   Another form of reality I guess.
And it really is a motivating factor because I was
hardworking like hell.   I really was.   Yup, the great
Gordon Gecko would've been real proud of me if he could've
seen me back then.   You see… I never did much study work
at high school, always did just enough to get through, but

I really tried hard those first couple of weeks at the
university. I really did. You see I'm actually a lazy
kind of individual who hates studying, but I tell you I
gave everything I had in the first couple of weeks of
being a student. I even sat in the front row of my class
so that I could hear everything the lecturer told us. I
even made notes I tell you. Yup, those were exciting
times and I really had good fun while I was there.

I got bored though. Hmm… pretty quickly actually. You
see… the first and second month of university was nice and
it opened up my eyes and everything. It definitely did.
But that was also about all Alvy CLEMENS could give. He
just couldn't do it month after month after month you
know. He figured it too boring and repetitive. As the
weeks dragged by, slowly but surely he started to move up
and up the class seats. Eventually he got to sit right at
the back with all the other students you know that are
smoking all kinds of horrible stuff. And he… he just
didn't bother anymore you see. Poor me Alvy CLEMENS.
    Didn't care.
    There… there at the back of class we talked about
everything except being a stockbroker. We were like
philosophers there at the back of the class and besides

being a philosopher in class and all, I… I remember how I
stared out of the open windows in class whilst dreaming
all kinds of things that had nothing to do with being a
poor student. That was the best.

Still, the whole university business is not as easy as
it looks. Not a catwalk. Definitely not a TV commercial
that's for sure. Especially when all the excitement of
being at a university and all that goes with being a first
year student disappears. After the excitement you kind of
realize that this is going to be real hard work.

You see… you ought to study at a university, real hard
too also and that's what I didn't like; picking up heavy
books and try figuring out what the hell were going on in
them because… because eventually you'll start puking over
the craziness of it all. I'm guess I'm just not one of
those people that do things such as picking up heavy books
and figuring them out. Gosh, I just wanted to be a
stockbroker and three or four years of having to study
myself into pieces for a lousy degree sounded a bit too
depressing for me. Just not relevant enough I thought.
Of course, my university psychologist believed I was nuts.
He diagnosed me with some kind of bipolar disorder.

'What's that?' I asked him.

'Bipolar disorder. It's a chemical imbalance in the

brain,' he said. 'Very common nowadays. Churchill had
it. Plato too. Don't even mention Socrates. He was full
of bipolar. Cicero was bipolar II. Napoleon was Bipolar
I. That's the extreme type. So too Hemingway. Then
there's…'

'But what's my type?'

'I don't know. Are you extreme?'

'I guess,' I said.

'Good,' he said. 'I have established you suffer from
bipolar mood disorder type 1.'

That's… that's how I was diagnosed with the damn
disease. Chemical imbalance in my brain. Today I figure
therapists make out all people to be mentally ill. When I
was younger I was said to have Aspergers' Syndrome.
Whatever that is.

'Listen mister, I don't feel mentally ill. I really
don't. I just want to drop out of university because it
makes me sick. The whole course I believe is irrelevant
to my ambition.'

'What do you mean by not relevant?'

'It's not relevant to my higher ambition,' I told him,
trying to sound clever and all. 'I want to be a
stockbroker, understand? Not a damn academic.'

'And now suddenly it's not relevant? Oh, but that's

absurd! Adult education is a wonderful experience Alvy CLEMENS. Especially in the 21stcentury. And for your information Mr. CLEMENS, everything we teach, everything you see here, believe me it's relevant.'

'Okay, then I guess I'm more into the irrelevant stuff of life. You know, things that don't appeal to anyone.'

'Oh, but we have irrelevance as well.'

'You do?'

'Naturally. We have some great irrelevant courses in Greek, not to mention their ancient irrelevant history.'

'The Greeks are irrelevant?' I asked.

'Well, is Paris a city?'

'Eh… sure. Why?'

'Then there you have it Alvy. Irrelevance is a Greek invention, in its purest…'

That psychologist went on and on about the irrelevance of Greek and he kind of lost me there too. He looked greedy anyhow and I suppose he wanted me to stay, fail, but still pay while failing. Anyway, I didn't pay attention to the phony and his pointless remarks. I just wanted to leave. And it's not only due to me not enjoying stockbroking and all. The whole university way of living I remember got on my nerves too after a while. The whole freaking system I tell you.

Gee, it was a real bore that university.

The beginning was nice yeah, but later on, oh, I don't even want to think about it. But… but to be short about it, you… you kind of realize after a couple of short weeks that you're just another student that wakes up early in the morning to see the face of an ugly lecturer. The lecturer, he or a she it doesn't matter, they drove me nuts. Especially when they kept on saying things like,

'Let… let me assure everyone: You have made a great career move by coming to this class. Remember: if you keep on working hard and attend classes every day, you'll become a great stockbroker!'

I mean, attend classes every day! Who does that? And… and if there's one thing that I hate more than anything, it's those damn lecturers.

Don't ask me why.

Boy, the girls at the university made it even worse for me there and I figure that's probably the main reason why I left. Yup. You see… the whole five date business that I told you about just now? It worked once I admit that, but it's not my kind a cup a tea if you know what I'm saying. No, that's just not who I am.

Let me put it this way. First, I had to be friends with the girl I wanted out on a date. Then, then I had to be friends with her friends, and, their friends' friends and then the girl, her friends, their friends' friends, together with Alvy CLEMENS, can go out together to watch a motion picture or go to a bar or to the same whatever it is that makes them tick. It was insane. All I wanted was to make out with the girl whilst the picture was playing and then work my way downward at the end of the night. However, that's not how the university girls operate, for they have a whole selection process. It's a heck of a process I tell you. Full of complications and everything and if you don't fit into that process of theirs it's practically game over and one may just as well check into a damn monastery because you're not going to see any real action soon I promise you. That's the university for you.

To make matters more difficult, I was a very poor guy back then. I'm still poor. But… my TV commercial days were completely suspended, reason being that I wasn't the flavour of the month. Gee, even the pornography people weren't much interested. Apparently they found some new guy, quite talented and all. The real thing they told me back then. He even got a scholarship to Amsterdam as an apprentice to better his craft.

Anyway, my mother hardly gave me any decent pocket money and it was damn frustrating times for me. So I couldn't afford any prostitutes like some of the other guys I know managed to do. I know, prostitutes are bad and all that, but I still figure them to be good company when I'm a bit lonely.

And it's not as if I'm not a good-looking guy. To tell you the truth, I'm blessed with good looks. I really am. Hell, I starred in a damn TV commercial, a best-seller of a TV commercial.

I left that place, but there was one final thing I had to think about before leaving for good. That of Gordon Gecko. What about my dream, my life as a billionaire? What happened to that?

To tell you the truth, I didn't see anyone at that university that wanted to be like Gordon Gecko. Not a single student. There were no higher ambitions at that place, no prospects of becoming famous or anything. I figured that not even the great Gordon Gecko would have stood for all that university crap. 'No sir,' he would've said, 'Get out of that wretched place and be a stockbroker on your own Alvy CLEMENS!' And that's what I did, although I didn't fancy anymore stockbroking.

I never would've made it in any case at university. Never in a million years. I don't belong there. So I

left the university without any trace of ever being there.
Except of course for being diagnosed a bipolar disorder.

'At least you did manage to shatter a few academic
records,' some idiot with glasses told me afterwards.
'Hypothetically speaking I should say.'

'Eh?'

'Well, let's face it Alvy. You're… you're a real hero.
A kind of a legendary character around campus.'

'Come again?'

'No… eh… Alvy CLEMENS. You really an infamous
character around here you know. We all admire your
courage for following your dreams.'

'What dreams?'

'Throwing your life away!'

I manhandled that courageous right there and I gave him
a good beating that last day on campus. He never knew
what was coming to him. Poor bastard.

He had a point though and I gave him credit for that
afterwards. You see, I shattered academic records for the
wrong reasons while I was there at that university place.
I failed everything, and, as a failure I suppose I was
indeed a legendary character.

I especially remember the disappointment I saw on my
mother's bipolar face the day I came home telling her

about it. I was very tired that day and it was warm like
hell. My mother was busy in the kitchen with the dishes
and all. My mother's, she's not that pretty you know, but
don't worry though, I don't feel like getting descriptive
with her today.

   'Oh Alvy!'

   'They say the bipolar made me do it. It's not even
me.'

   'And what about Uncle Lennie? What… what did he say?'

   My mother almost started crying right there. My mother
looks like a gypsy, right. But the way she cries? Hell,
she looks like a stroke victim.

   'And how could you?'

   'How could I?'

   'Yes, how could you?'

   'Don't know,' I said. 'You said I've got character,
didn't you? Well, I'm still figuring the character part
out.'

   'Not on my expense you don't. Damn you!'

   My mother then eventually said something like hmm…,
'Now don't you get funny with me Alvy! Don't you! You're
on your own now. Yes. All on your own in this damn
world.' Something like that. I never pay much attention.

   I helped my mother in the kitchen whilst pondering the

whole matter through like a university academic. My mother, she loves me a lot I know and I figure she wanted me to turn into just like Uncle Lennie's sons, Ronnie and Joe, smart and all. But like I said I'm not like that. I wanted to do my own thing.

Don't make a mistake; I was disappointed about stockbroking.

All that thanks to that crazy Gordon Gecko and his depressing <u>Wall Street</u> movie and also great thanks to Oliver Stone and Michael Douglas and every one who was involved in that movie.

Thanks.

Thanks for nothing.

Chapter Five

Believe me, I wasn't discouraged. Nah, not at all I tell

you. I don't get discouraged that easily. For it was

that Hemingway 'character' who got me on my feet again.

Well, they say he had character. You know him, don't you?

Yeah, the guy who wrote books and stuff and I… I don't

read many books.

    Actually, I hate it.

    I can't stand it and if I think of it, I've read only

about five books on my own in my entire life. I read Tom

Sawyer and Huckleberry Finn a few times. A couple of

Harry Potter books also, but that's about it. Books don't

interest me really. My dad once muttered that books are

for homosexuals. That's probably the cleverest thing I

ever heard anyone say.

    However, if there's… if there's one book that really

got me thinking, then it's that The Old Man and the Sea

whom that Hemingway guy wrote. It was my Uncle Lennie's

book and I remember how bored I was that day at his house

watching television.

    Oh, I didn't mention Uncle Lennie. He was my best

friend, my best grown-up friend I should say. He really

was a peach of an uncle. He really was, but he died of

cancer just a couple of months of ago, (a few days after
Christmas in fact) like my dad. They were brothers.
That's the CLEMENS's genes for you. Full of poison.

Anyway, Uncle Lennie, he was a cheese-maker. Yeah, he
made cheese for a living. Had a whole factory and
everything. He was an old man, one of my best friends.
Unbelievable. Ah, and then there's, well… then there's
Ronnie and Joe, his two sons. My nephews. I don't like
them that much. They're too intellectual for me.

Ronnie, he… he is the older brother. I remember
beating the crap out him once because he made fun of me.
Asshole. I really think he's a Satanist or something. He
is just such a bad person, that Ronnie. So negative on
life. Joe, he's some philosophy student. Very clever
also. He's always busy quoting some philosopher. Always
busy on the meaning of life and crap. Not my cup of tea
either, but, we spent a lot of time together the three of
us, because of Uncle Lennie. We had many laughs together
also, and… they know me pretty well.

Anyway, so I went over to my uncle's to watch the TV
you know and there was this little book lying on top of
the TV set, The Old Man And The Sea, right? So I read the
first few pages just out of curiosity. A couple of hours
later, I finished the whole book. Gosh, it killed me, the

book that is. It gives me goose bumps just thinking about
it. Then I heard from my best friend Roger that Hemingway
also won the Nobel Prize in writing books. So it's not as
if he was just one of those crazy people who became famous
for his personal way of life than what he actually
achieved in life. That rather impressed me and The Old
Man and the Sea for me is proof of that.

    Especially where the old man in the book keeps
wondering about the great Di Maggio and what the great Di
Maggio would have done in the old man's shoes and also how
the old man struggled for days to kill that big fish and…
and when he finally did managed to cut the fish's throat
or something like that, the bloody sharks came and ate the
fish all up and all that time the old man kept thinking
about the great Di Maggio. Terrific.

    I don't know if you know about Joe Di Maggio, but he
was a legendary baseball player that played for the New
York Yankees. I'm told that he smashed all kinds of
records. Gee, I don't know how baseball works, it looks
very much like cricket to me, but if the old man liked it,
then… then I'll probably like it as well.

    'Now Hemingway,' Uncle Lennie told me. 'If ever there
was a nutcase in life, it's him. Quite a character too.
I remember that he once…'

'What do you mean by character?' I interrupted.

'Well,' my uncle explained, 'to put the word 'nutcase' mildly...'

'I mean character!' My uncle's hearing was terrible.

'Yes, to put the word 'character' in historical perspective, Hemingway shot his own brains to pieces, eh... little fragments.'

'He did?'

'Yup.'

'But...'

'Although I must admit that he was very sick when he did what he did and I know he was a heavy drunk also. Drank himself to pieces sometimes.'

'Sounds rough.'

'Had trouble with woman too I remember. I don't think he was a depressive character; he just liked living like on the edge. But definitely a character. Definitely.'

'Sounds like that manic-depression thing my psychologist was on about,' I said.

'Heh?'

'I said it sounds like that manic-depression...'

'No no, I don't believe in these psychologists or psychiatrists or whatever these things are. Hemingway was a gifted man of character. It's funny, they say he died honorably.'

'Honorably?'

'Ah, honorably yes. Like a truly great artist they say. He lived for his work, and, ah, he died for it too.'

Honorably I say.

But now you know… that's where my obsession with this whole Hemingway character started. With a book. And then… then I also started dreaming about it and I love dreaming. I'm not joking. It's brilliant. Much better than celebrating a birthday alone. All the things that I can't do during the day, all the people that I cannot beat the crap out of, all the frustrations I've got to deal with. In my dreams I'm a madman, an animal in fact.

It's a brilliant gift, dreaming.

So when I finished reading that book, that eh… <u>Old Man And The Sea</u> one, I kept on dreaming about it, as if I was the old man himself. Then I found out about Hemingway, about all the crazy things he did in his life and, how he managed to get himself killed. Can you believe that?

He shot himself with a shotgun. No sweat.

And right there… that's where I decided I was going to be like him.

You want to know my dreams of Hemingway right?

Fine.

Let's see… most of the time I dreamt of him, I dreamt of him being this huge rough bearded guy with a scruffy voice that did all kinds of brave and wonderful things on his own in the jungle and when he came back from doing all his wonderful things he would sit down, get drunk and say something like, 'Well, I suppose it won't hurt to write all this down on a piece of paper. I suppose it would make a pretty good story. Ha-ha!'

In my crazy dreams, I remember how I saw Hemingway walking towards me back from his hunting trips carrying some one-eyed beast over his shoulders. He didn't remove the insides of the beast out there in the bushes where I couldn't see. No, he had to carry the beast with its insides and everything back to the hut where I was waiting and only when he saw me at the hut waiting he would start removing the insides as if I enjoyed seeing him do it.

Then, after carefully removing the insides, he would chop off the beast's ivory horns with his axe that he carried with. He would skin the beast with some expensive imported Swiss knife, time to time licking the salty blood from the shiny blade; as if he'd done it a million times before! He'll tie the beast up on a rope and he would gaze at it for a long long time. Then… then he would see me staring and he'll ask me in that scruffy voice of his,

'What, you never see someone do this kind of thing before?'

'No…'

'What's your problem, boy?'

'Eh… Mr. Hemingway,' I'll say to him, 'it's just that, err, you're that Hemingway guy.'

'What do you mean? Defend yourself!'

'Eh… you're a famous person. What I mean is, you… you write books and stuff. You're not supposed to go off hunting and killing huge one-eyed beasts just to make yourself feel good. You've got character.'

'Hmm…'

He frowned at me and then said, 'Interesting point you have there, Alvy CLEMENS. I guess you're right. Thanks for the advice,' and then for some old reason he would get depressed about what I told him and that's when he started to drink and write as if he had just gone mad. Some crazy dream, eh?

There was this other one too. A kind of a nightmare dream.

'Forget it Alvy CLEMENS! You don't have what it takes to be like me.'

'Oh I have. Just… just you wait and see… Mr.

Hemingway. Just you wait…'

'This is the 21st century Alvy CLEMENS. Go find some real work.'

'I don't want to,' I told him. 'I… I choose my own destiny.'

'Ha, you watch way too much television, Alvy. That's what's wrong with you 21st century people. That's right. Hmm… yes… no wonder only scientists believe we are descendents from the apes.'

'Eh?'

'See what I mean Alvy boy? 21st century people are supposed to change the world and everything. They don't think. Goodness.'

'I think.'

'Yes, about the size of your penis. Ha, that's very thoughtful.'

'Shut up Hemingway! I got bipolar too!'

'I had no bipolar. Bipolar are for homosexuals! I hate homos… ha ha! Don't worry, Alvy CLEMENS,' he bellowed while puffing on his old pipe. 'I mean no harm. Ha, I've done myself in already!'

The dream wasn't very encouraging, I admit. But like I said, I don't get discouraged.

Gosh, I got so obsessed with Hemingway at some stage

that I decided to do everything he once did. My best
friend Roger said that Hemingway was also a sports
journalist at some point in time. So I figured, after
dropping out of university and all, I could do that for a
year or so, a bit of sports journalism, covering all sorts
of sports. I knew my sports pretty well but I didn't want
to do it for the rest of my life if you know what I mean.

Then, if I would be so lucky, I'd do some traveling
like an old bum and see the world, maybe go to Cuba or
Spain and do a bit of deep sea fishing and game hunting,
learn to bullfight and cockfight. Even… even learn to box
properly. All the things he once did.

Then, hopefully, if we get another world war or
something, I'd like to be one of those reporters in the
fighting. Who knows, maybe I can do a bit of combat
fighting myself.

When I'm finished with that, I'll write about all the
things I've done. I'd give all my writing to some
publisher and if he likes it, he can put it all into a
book and publish it, so that all the rich and clever
people can read and discuss it. Then, when that's done
and I'm all old and sick and ready to die, I'll take my
own life.

Even the crazy Romans say it's the best way a man can

die.

I mean, what's the point in keeping a person alive when he's better off dead in any case?

But now you know… that's what I all figured back then. First, to be a journalist, a great one of course. Then, to do some traveling and then… then to tell every one of what an interesting life I had.

Chapter Six

I'm probably one of those guys that complain about every little damn thing, more so being today my birthday, but I tell you; it's all for good reason. My advice: be patient.

My Hemingway career went smooth and starting out I thought that when I become a journalist, I would go out there and get that juicy story. My boss would congratulate me on what a great job I've done. I'll tell him of other stories I'm working on and my boss would keep on congratulating me saying,

'Gee, you're a great journalist, the best one in my staff!

'Keep up the good work old Alvy!' he'll tell me and I would get the journalist of the year award and every newspaper editor in the country would come up to me and ask,

'Listen Alvy, we need a great journalist in our staff.'

'Why me?'

'Why you? Cause you're simply the most accomplished journalist around that's why Alvy CLEMENS. Face the facts.'

'But… but I'm hardly qualified,' I'll tell him.

'It doesn't matter, Alvy,' he'll start again. 'Say, who here make the best cup of coffee?' and gosh, all I had to do was to make coffee. Gosh.

Seriously and I mean it, journalists today just sit there like unexcited machines with their damn computers in front of them, with all the latest programs on it and work there for most of the day, with their strong cups of coffee of course. I was there and it's a real mission just trying to stay awake. Only when a nice girl walks by, then you'd sit up and have a nice look at her backside, but then suddenly, you realize that you're actually getting paid to do some work.

Sometimes they'll ask you to go out and listen to an 'important' press conference or interview some big shot famous guy, but journalism is not as exciting as I thought it would be. You just sit there in those small depressive cubicles with all the funny looking computers and get frustrated like hell.

Like I said, it's depressing.

And it gives me a real headache.

They say that Hemingway reported on the whole world war as an ambulance driver and being in the fighting and all of that. Now that's exciting. I don't care about the dangers just as long as I get excited about my work.

Otherwise I'll start seeing prostitutes and get frustrated like hell.

I was still very young at the time of being a journalist. I practically did it for free, (I was one of those, what do you call it, those 'interns') so I did some other things too, criminal things, which was a little more exciting and rewarding. It kind a kept me from going insane if you know what I mean.

But it really is tough to keep a straight face about everything I just told you about, with the big corporations and all, especially when one keeps on doing the same sort of boring work, day in and day out. You should know how it feels when you do something everyday that you… you just don't enjoy. I hate it more than anything else. You start questioning all kinds of things you never did before and that's when you lose your head and start drinking in the middle of the day and go to one of those run down prostitutes that makes one feel like committing suicide. It really gets to you.

We don't get to do much investigative journalism anymore, like they had with that Kennedy, you know… the guy who got assassinated. Then there was this whole conspiracy surrounding it.

Personally I'm very big on the whole Kennedy

assassination. I know every little detail about it - the day it occurred, the number of shots fired, where it was fired from, the type of gun used, the single bullet theory. I even watched that picture, <u>JFK</u>, it's pretty good I tell you. I'm a Kennedy expert. I can go on about it for hours.

Most of the time though the big corporations have all the fun by doing the Kennedy investigations for us. We just have to type it up and there you have it. We're not allowed to ask why. What's the fun in all that? Getting up early to go to work for the satisfaction of only a small paycheck is just not enough for an energetic guy like Alvy CLEMENS.

Maybe…

Maybe when I get married and when I've got to look after my children, I'll do that kind of work just because of the money and the security and all that stuff grown-ups lose sleep over.

But I really don't think about being a grown-up too often, I really don't. I get headaches if I do think about it.

Chapter Seven

About Kennedy, everybody's on it being a conspiracy and all. You probably know more than I do.

Everybody and I mean everybody goes on and on about it being a conspiracy and all and how the government assassinated Kennedy.

I don't buy that kind of crap to such an extent.

You see… Harvey Lee Oswald got a bit mental and everything. Kind of lonely and frustrated. He wanted some company, wanted a bit of attention, right? Forget about his involvement regarding the KGB for just a moment. I personally find it not so relevant.

Personally, and I mean personally, assassinating the most powerful man in the world isn't such a bad idea to get some attention. Loneliness is hell and you know… sometimes, hell is other people, meaning that there's people out there who remain lonely whatever their circumstances. Hence mental illness. But there you go. I figure Harvey Lee wanted to make himself happy in… in another metaphysical way of some sorts, getting in touch with his <u>Spider-Man</u> or something. That's my single bullet theory. No damn conspiracy.

If I was to assassinate our President and I mean if, I

would do it for a good and honorable cause you know, not just to make myself feel good. I'm not fed up with life you know. No yet in any case.

Anyway, I fled the journalism world in a hurry because I felt that everybody was conspiring against me. But that's life. A damn conspiracy. I then started to do some writing on my own. Eh, what do you call it? Writing for the soul, that crap. Then… then I realize there's nothing much to write about, except about myself and I hated writing about myself all the time. Too damn boring. I also had the funny feeling that no one was ever going to see the things that I was putting to paper and in South Africa especially, telling someone that you write and stuff is like telling him you're Woody Allen or somebody famous no one sees or knows or hear about.

'I'm a writer nowadays,' I remember telling my older nephew Ronnie once.

'A what?'

'You know, I write and stuff,' I told him.

'Uh-uh, you, you mean you're a bum,' he said.

'No.'

'Yes, you're an unemployed bum; you hate yourself because you can't get decent work and now you're sitting

in your room all day long trying to figure out what is
wrong with you by writing some depressing crap only you
like reading.'

'Kind a like that,' I said.

'Well, then you're not a writer,' he said.

'What am I then?' I wanted to know.

'Well, to be honest here, you're a psychopath that's
what you are Alvy CLEMENS. A ticking time bomb ready to
explode any second.'

'See Alvy. You're a headcase. Mentally ill.
Dementia…'

I remember beating the crap out of him while he was
busy phrasing that dementia sentence and I broke his nose
and everything and he made a real scene of it also. Said
I wanted to kill him.

I definitely should've.

And… you know what's funny? He's four years older than
me, that Ronnie. No kidding. I just hate intellectuals
and their glasses. Gosh, I had to get the madman a new
pair of glasses.

He… he had a good point though, just like the other
deadbeat guy with glasses at university had a good point.
My writing wasn't and still isn't anything special. Won't
win the Nobel Prize or anything. I don't think someone

like Shakespeare would've start shaking in his boots.

Then… then I figured of going to the movies and writing screenplays for a change. Sounds wonderful, eh? But then I realize that no one makes motion pictures in this country. I knew this guy from school who was always busy writing scripts for films. He loved doing it, he practically got a haemorrhage doing it, but it didn't work out for him in the end.

Poor guy.

He's probably doing some crappy job nobody wants right now.

Well, I'm not sure what's wrong with the arts and culture sides of things here in the southern points of Africa because creative people like artists and writers or whatever you want to call them… they don't get a lot of encouragement these days. What do you do then? I understand. I really do. You have so many millions who can't find work because they've got either the HIV, or they're either too stupid, or there's no work for them and now these crazy creative bipolar guys who call themselves sexually frustrated artists too starts complaining. I don't expect them not to complain, but still… it's a depressing thought.

That's why, with all that's going on around here, I've

The Real Yahoo.   Bruwer, H

been doing some serious thinking. You know… about going
away for a while you know, do some traveling and see the
world. All that stuff. I had a chance of going overseas
with my best friend Roger once and I'll tell you more
about it later, but as with most things, it didn't work as
I pictured it in my head. I still would love to go. If I
get the opportunity.

Maybe I'd get the chance to live like Robinson Crusoe
for a few years when I eventually do go overseas. I've
always thought about that. It would be a nice adventure,
learning to take care of myself and build my own little
paradise in the middle of bloody nowhere. I'll make
friends with the islanders and we can build our own
civilization, our own damn world. That is if I can fit
all of it in.

Maybe… if all goes well, I'd get the chance to meet
Friday along the way. Just… just like it's supposed to
be, and, every full moon we'll prepare to fight off the
cannibals in their canoes and every time they get all
comfortable in their canoes and all, we'll kick their ass
back to where it came from and… and I'll return after a
few years as a wise and a brave man going on about my
adventures as if I'm the great Robinson Crusoe himself.

A true hero.

And then Friday and me can talk about our adventures to they who wants to listen about it.

'Me and Friday had a ball,' I'll tell them all. 'Yeah, those full moons were tough, real tough I tell you, but... I still had fun. It's like trying out a new therapist. You really should give it a go,' and they... they who want to listen about it would hopefully learn, really learn from Friday and me. Admire us too of course.

'Oh, thank you Mr. CLEMENS!

'My, you're so clever. Thank you Alvy CLEMENS!'

'Alvy for President!'

'Alvy Robinson Crusoe CLEMENS!

Yes, that's me, Alvy Robinson Crusoe/Bipolar CLEMENS. And maybe they can use our advice to do something useful, maybe build this universe for a change instead of destroying it.

I'm not saying this because I want to be funny and I'd like to impress you of how I know Robinson Crusoe and Friday, those two are no big deal trust me, but... but I really mean what I'm saying about getting away because it's not fun being a citizen sometimes. Yup, at some places, especially here in Brooklyn, one feels trapped. That's how difficult it is to make a living nowadays. Sometimes I guess, you just need to get away from it all.

Hmm, I wonder what that old Hemingway would have said about it, if he really thought about anything at all. He was still probably chasing that big fish and thinking about the great Di Maggio before he got to think what I'm thinking.

But hey, life is not a thinking contest, nor about catching a big old fish. Hemingway got it wrong. He should start his whole book all over again.

PART TWO

Chapter Eight

FRIDAY AFTERNOON

You know how Cape Town looks early in the morning, especially in the summer where everybody's already at work and the only thing you can do is sit outside and inhale the smoky air? Well, if it weren't for the breeze coming from the sea we'll all probably die of lung cancer or something. That's how polluted the sky can get.

Don't get me wrong, Cape Town is a nice city. I mean… I can understand why people come here. We have brilliant weather, it's really terrific and then there's Table Mountain and Robben Island reminding us of our terrific past.

Tourists love this place and I can understand why. You know… I've never ever been up that mountain. Yeah I know. I'm a big disappointment.

Today is very hot by the way. When it's this hot, my mom tends to get an epileptic seizure due to the poisonous smoke coming from the factories across our neighborhood. Luckily, she's not here. Yup, she's gone out with that Michael K. boyfriend of hers for the day. It's Friday so she's not working. She promised though to cook me a nice meal for supper because… because it's my birthday and all.

Where was I? Oh, I forgot. My silly life. Well, I was at a dead end back then. Things didn't work out. The whole being famous thing I had planned, well, it kind of blew up in my face.

I was staying at home.

I had no ambition, nothing.

I didn't feel like getting a job, but I also didn't feel like getting into trouble, like stealing a box of chocolates, something I like doing.

No, I was just sitting around the house smoking cigarettes all day long whilst waiting for my mother to come back from her fascinating temporary job as a social worker. I tell you, she gets these sudden impulses to help mental people, yet she's the manic-depressive.

My Uncle Lennie, he lived a few blocks away from us, I visited him often but he was out on another damn holiday so there was nobody besides him that I felt that would make me happy. My mother was about the only good friend I had. She's not that a bad company, but you see, you can only talk so much with her.

'Oh Alvy, I wonder what the weather will be like tomorrow. It's freezing today.'

'Hmm...'

'What do you say Alvy?'

'About what?'

'Don't get cute with me Alvy CLEMENS!'

'Relax mom. It's supposed to be freezing and all.
It's winter.'

'I know it is the darn winter, but oh…, still, I do
hope the sun will shine tomorrow.'

By the way, it's not really winter, but that's my
mother's favorite topic of discussion, the damn weather.
And global warming. I mean, what does she know about
global warming? You see… you can't ask my mother out for
a beer or anything like that. You can't ask her if
whether she thinks Hustler or Playboy is the better
magazine.

                    *   *   *

Anyway, I do enjoy motion pictures I really do. I don't
like many things, you know that by now, but if there's one
thing that I do like, then it's motion pictures.
Especially mob ones.

    I remember how I got to watch all the classics from
when it was still the black and white pictures and then
when my dad didn't mind me hearing the f-words and
watching the sex, I started to watch the more violent ones

with all the blood and sex in the colour pictures and from
there on in I just kept on seeing gangster pictures. I
can go on telling you about it for hours. I'm really a
nutcase when it comes to these pictures. I still… I still
am you know. If you'd ask me how many times I watched all
of Tarantino and Scorsese's motion pictures, you'll think
I'm crazy. So I won't tell, but I can assure you it was
many a time because I've memorized it all in my head.

   And… and not only those two you know. Others also I
remember. Every week I would see a new gangster picture
and for the rest of the week I'll pretend as if I'm in
that picture in reality; until I see another picture the
following week that I also like.

   I remember how I played out the pictures in my head at
night when I couldn't fall sleep and when I finally did
fell asleep, I dreamt I was one of those guys in the
pictures with the black hat and smoky cigar in the mouth.
I tell you it was a bit like having a nightmare. Then I
would be too damn scared to get out of my bed the next day
because I felt that when I opened that door, those
gangsters I disobeyed in my dream are going to wait for me
with their pistols and shotguns. (I saw Keyser Soze in
real life I swear.)

   If I think back to it now, I maybe took it all a bit

too seriously because I've done some pretty bad things in my life.

Do you remember that scene in <u>Goodfellas</u> where Ray Liotta tells Joe Pesci of how funny he was and how Joe Pesci nearly wanted to bite his freaking head off because he thought that Ray Liotta was making him out to be a freaking clown?

Or… or that scene in <u>The Soprano's</u> where Christopher and Paulie were chasing after some mad Russian in the woods and how Christopher lost his shoe in the snow and how he feared he was going to lose his foot because of it?

And how the two of them ate expired ketchup sachets for lunch in a freezing car and how they started to drive each other crazy, so much so that after a while they wanted to shoot each other's heads off?

Do you remember that scene?

It's terrific I know.

Well, that's what I love about the gangster pictures. You can actually learn from it. I may be wrong, but I think psychology plays a big role in these gangster pictures. It's hard to explain you knoe, but I feel like if I'm getting educated while watching it, like if I'm doing homework or doing something that is worthwhile.

I studied Freud a little at school and he's supposed to

be pretty high up in this psychology crap. But when I think of it, the only good thing that Freud really taught me was something regarding sex.

A real necessity.

Still, I've always felt that watching these gangster pictures make me a smarter person. Not like these big budget Jerry Bruckheimer crap we get to see all the time. It's sickening. How he manages to spend so much money on a single motion picture, only he knows. He must have been an explosive expert before he started making pictures because that's all I ever get to see in his pictures.

Big explosions.

Big explosions.

How boring can you get?

Me, if I watch stuff like that, if I dare to, I'd stick to the low-budget formula with Chuck Norris or Dolph Lundgren in it. Why? Because they… they don't want to impress you with special effects or big explosions. They tell the story as it is. They're not the best of actors, they're awful I know, but it's better fun watching them act like idiots than seeing this Bruckheimer trying to impress you of what a great explosive expert he once was.

Boy, the guy's a complete peach, a real Yahoo and on top of that, he takes some big name actor along with him

and then everyone goes on of what a great director he is.
I don't like to be impressed by other people, especially
not a guy like Jerry Bruckheimer. He knows nothing at all
about psychology or anything else for that matter.

Anyway, I'm probably driving you nuts by now. I
apologize. I really do. It's not normal to go and on
about all my crazy ideas. I really do apologize if I'm
boring you.

The Real Yahoo.   Bruwer, H

Chapter Nine

Anyway, a deep love for the pictures could only mean one
thing back then. The episode after the Hemingway debacle…
oh, that's where I met the President, at that film school
I went to. Oh sorry. I'm confusing you. There's this
film school in Cape Town, right? And I, I just wanted to
make movies at that place when all of a sudden it happened
and I met the President and it was good fun. Apparently,
he's son went there too. I'm not kidding. I never saw
the guy there to be honest.

The President's son I mean.

But, the way it occurred, the President, he wanted to
check the place out you know, to see if it's any good for
his son and all. Then, all of a sudden, while fiddling
with the cameras and crap, I heard noises in the corridor,
people suddenly going unconscious because the President
was supposedly in the house and I… I always wanted to meet
and talk to the President.

Anyway, Alvy CLEMENS nearly faked a heart attack in the
corridor of the film school's acting department just in
order to speak to the President. It was quite a sight you
know, seeing the President in the flesh. For a moment I
thought that the President's bodyguards eyed me

suspiciously, but as I said, I faked a heart attack, and after I recovered, we… we had a chat. Gee, what an impressive character!

'Are you feeling good now?'

'Err… Alvy CLEMENS.'

'Are you feeling well?'

'Yes, yes… my name is Alvy CLEMENS. I'm in charge here.'

'And… do you enjoy this place?'

'Love it,' I said. 'It's just… just brilliant Mr. President. It really is.'

'That's good.'

'We'll take good care of your son. We won't repeat the Kennedy's, trust me.'

'Heh? Oh good,' he said. 'Yes, that's good.'

'Although I do think Mr. President, after studying the never-seen-before footage, the possibility of a second, third, even fourth shooter is now a definite possibility.'

'Possibility?'

'Yes, and I also don't think we should by all means exclude the possibility of a possible coup to overthrow the United States government. However…'

'Hmm,' he said, real diplomatically. 'I do think you make a good point regarding something there. Well done eh... CLEMENS that you right?'

'Oh, yes. I'm CLEMENS. That's me alright.'

'Are you feeling fine now?'

'Eh...

'Take care,' and he left with his bodyguards and all his diplomatic servants. He looked like goddamn sultan.

Anyway, we didn't have an intellectual or philosophical discussion or anything and we definitely didn't go on about the weather. I made sure of that.

No, it was just a nice... a nice moment of general discussion I should say.

Let's jump to that film school in the city. I mean about what I did while I was there after I decided to take the course.

Well, I learned a lot. I really did this time. And... trust me. Making motion pictures? It's not as simple as it looks. Nah, not at all. You... you can't just go out there and start shooting the scenes left right and center just for the hell of it. No, you have to draw up some plan first, kind of an agenda, and only then decide what you want in the scene and what angle you should use and all that stuff. It really gets complicated after a while. You... you have to have your wits about you when it comes to

making motion pictures. I tell you, it's not as easy as
it looks.

I hated though to look into the video camera itself. I
hated it back when I was big shot TV commercial star and I
still hate it today.

Gosh I hate the camera.

Even the one that takes photos. It makes me so damn
conscious of myself. I can understand why they invented
it, but I still hate it.

My mother, she has this family album at home and I used
to go sometimes and have a look at it to see if I really
did look so silly when I was still a kid and I tell you,
every time I saw myself on that photo album I felt like
throwing up. I really do.

And… when they asked me to look into that video camera
of theirs, all those memories of my TV commercial days and
of my mother's family album flooded back into my damn
memories.

I just wanted to puke to my guts out.

I told them I've got this thing about cameras and all;
that it kind of freaked me out. Made me nervous and
everything. But there was this guy with the ugliest
teeth, and… and who dressed up like a girl and everything
and he squealed in my ear,

'All right, CLEMENS I get it. You're a little nervous.
But… but this is showbiz buddy.'

   'Showbiz?' I asked.   'What the heck is that?'

   'Yup. Yeah, buddy,' he said. 'This is what we call
showbiz and we don't get nervous and all.'   Luckily the
homosexual didn't touch me and I didn't get to see much of
him and that was nice. But… but the other prostitutes at
the film school, they just shoved me in front of that damn
thing. They probably thought that this tall good-looking
fellow with dark hair is a born actor or something. But I
tell you, I stood there like Woody Allen, looking as if I
was ready to wet my pants any second. I tell you it's
scary. Trying to look into that little pee-hole and give
painful smiles just to show that it isn't such a big deal.
They put me in front of that thing for over five minutes.
They explained that if I ever wanted to make great films I
should have a sound knowledge of acting and its different
forms of challenges. Something like that. I was so
embarrassed after that episode I promised myself never to
go back there again.

   I finished the whole course, because I paid for it and
all. My mother and I was struggling with the money sides
of things and for me just to quit because I hated to look
it into a stupid video camera sounded a bit silly. I

figured that it would be dumb for me to waste the money if
I already paid for it. Besides, I had nothing to do back
then.

At that time I was just one of those guys who kept
hanging around at those crappy bars, those unemployed bars
you get during the middle of the day where everyone goes
on about how lucky they are not to work and how nice it is
to be a free man. I remember how everyone in those bars
would go on about it.

'Isn't life great,' one worthless guy will say, 'no
responsibilities, no worries, no concerns, just every man
for himself.'

'No,' someone else will say, 'it's not every man for
himself. Every man lives for himself!'

'No,' some other guy will say, 'it's not every man
lives for himself. Man makes himself!'

'Yeah, let's drink to that,' everyone else will say.
'Man makes himself! Hurray!'

What a bunch of creepy Yahoos.

In fact, every time I went in there, everyone looked so
damn miserable about their lives as free unemployed men
and everything that you really had to see it to be believe
it. Every time I looked into the eyes of those fools I
thought they were going to start crying any second. I

tell you it's true. You had to see it to believe it.

Man makes himself my ass. They were all a bunch of
worthless characters and they probably still are.

Hmm… yes. There was also a real nice looking girl at
that film school. Hmm… yes. She was with me in class I
think. Very nice looking I tell you. Gee, I can't
remember her name, the nice looking girl that is. It was
quite a while back, more than a year ago in fact. But she
was very pretty and if it wasn't for her disappointing
face I promise you she would've been a highly paid
prostitute because she had a terrific body. She had
everything I remember correctly. It was just her face
that I didn't enjoy looking at. In fact, that face of
hers looked rather messy. I tell you, she probably got
stung by a swarm of bees when she was little or something.
It looked rather messy on the facial side.

If… if I could've taken her face off with some chainsaw
and replace it with some girl you see in the cover of
those woman magazines you get, I swear I would've done
that and married her, but… but she had a really nice body
and I was still pretty stiff and horny back then so I
didn't care much of how she looked like just as long as
she knew where I was coming from.

Anyway, I knew probably the least about filmmaking from everyone that was there. I mean it's only natural. I'm a novice, an amateur when it comes to making motion pictures.

But I was enthusiastic about it, more than all the assholes that were there combined. I also asked many a question and a lot of them were probably basic questions that I could've figured out on my own, but I asked it anyhow. What's the use of a lecturer, besides irritating the hell out of a madman, eh?

And it was not like in school where we got asked difficult questions or had to do hours of homework for the next day. No, it was very practical. Gee, I love practical stuff. It's brilliant.

I rather liked that practical approach. I didn't want to get embarrassed with questions that I didn't study the previous day at home. We got this huge stack of notes about filmmaking though and I remember paging through it a couple of times. But… but it's such an effort and I get distracted so easily. Whenever I see an ant crawling up my knee or something like that I start to play with the damn thing. For hours.

I'm crazy, I know.

I'm a lunatic to be precise.

Then, with all the excitement over and the ant
squashed, I'll throw aside my stack of notes and switch on
the TV and watch all kinds of meaningless programs all day
long instead of going through that notes I told you about.
To tell you the truth, my memory is terrible. You know…
my mom still doesn't want to enclose my IQ score. She
says she's afraid I'll do something stupid afterwards.
Maybe… maybe she has a point there. You never know how
the populations mentally ill will react on bad news.

Still, I did a lot while I was there at that film
school in the city. I really did. We watched dozens of
films, more than dozens, but most of them we're art films
and it didn't interest me much. Personally, I'm not very
big on art. It's too spooky. The lecturer though, in
true lecturer fashion of course, he kept on telling me,

'Art films Alvy, the best of the best. It's the
greatest of cinema. Oh, the French cinema. *C'est genial!*
It was and it will always be. Now… remember that next
time you wander off somewhere in your head old Alvy
CLEMENS.'

'Why should I remember it?'

'Because it's art Alvy. Art, great art especially,
will always be remembered. It's timeless.'

'Timeless?'

'Believe me.'

I scratched my head and said, 'All right. Art is timeless. Long live timeless art.'

I didn't want to argue with the guy. Art is not my subject anyway. But remember this:

Lecturers are like parents.

They're always right.

Even if they know they're wrong about something, they're still right.

One thing about lecturers though and I'm not joking when I'm saying this; Lectures are the greatest and biggest liars I've ever come across.

I swear.

They keep on fooling everybody.

Chapter Ten

To be honest, the thing I have for staring into video
cameras really crushed my spirits. I figured being a
full-time director. Then these film experts figured I
looked like some Dean actor. But I… I looked so pathetic
in front of that camera. I tell you, my Jewish nose
looked like the size of a football in front of that camera
and I specifically remember some ill nutcase who
deliberately laughed out loud when he saw my performance.
That same nutcase also had the guts to pat me in the back
and congratulate me of what a great character I am. I
mean, he doesn't even know what character is!

   I would've beaten the crap out of him if it weren't for
that nice looking girl with the ugly face who I've
mentioned before and who I was still trying to impress.

Jesus, that girl was such a waste in the end, so clingy
and all. I swear she would've wiped my butt if I asked
her to. It really was all worthless and after a while,
the only thing she talked about is relationship-
relationships. And I got real scared when that girl whose

name I can't remember mentioned anything about
relationships. Especially when she read it from those
woman magazines. You know… all that mumbo jumbo.

'Look what's written here,' she'll start with her
girlie voice. '*Confront your partner directly and ask him
to share his thoughts. Remember: Relationships is built
out of honesty and trust.*'

'What do you say your thoughts are Alvy?'

'Huh?'

'Oh Alvy… say something nice. Pretty please?'

See? That's how it started. Woman magazines.

'How many times don't I say you have a pretty face?
How many times?'

'Oh, what a big liar you are.   My face is full of
fungus. Everybody thinks that.'

'No, it's terrific I swear.'

'You're lying.'

'No.'

'Everyone say my face looks like a frozen pizza,'
she'll end up saying. She was right. It was the goddamn
truth. Her face looked disgusting, and I guess it really
contributed to her possessive character. I probably gave
her a lot of self-esteem.

'You're imagining things. It's beautiful.'

'I don't believe you.'

'Come… come on,' I'll tell her, trying to comfort her and everything. 'They're just acting jealous. It's perfectly normal for them to say that. Jealousy is a wonderful thing. Trust me, your friends are acting jealous cause you have a sexy boyfriend.'

'You serious?' she asked, 'I got a pretty face?'

'What? You're pretty like hell,' I kept on telling her.

'Oh, Alvy.'

Then she would keep her mouth shut for a few seconds and we'll start with each other's private parts and that's how it went with her. Don't, I tell you, don't get too cute with relationships because five seconds later she'll ask,

'Say something?'

'I'm thinking.'

'Why don't you talk to me?'

'I just did, but I like being alone now and then, thinking my own stuff. If you don't mind.'

A panic attack from her would follow, followed by a revision of all that relationship crap you know, sharing ones feelings and all that.

'I feel… I feel as though you're shutting me out Alvy

CLEMENS!'

Boy, don't get to cute with relationships, even if it's built on terrific lies. She was hard to please you know and I felt smothered and… and I wanted my freedom, like that Nelson Mandela character and I remember the day I started breaking up with the girl whose name I can't remember and how I regained my freedom.

It was terrible. For her I mean. I remember we had just finished having sex and I was still trying to catch my breath and all when she started to do that whole cuddle business with me as if I was her cute little pet or something. I know I'm real good-looking and darn irresistible and sometimes it makes feel great but… but I also don't need to be reminded of it every second of my life. She then got hold of my self-conscious Jewish nose, rubbing it, kissing it, molesting it even. How peachy is that? But… but she insisted on the whole cuddle thing.

'You know what, Alvy? You're so cute. So cute! I just love you!'

As you can expect, all her relationship talk was driving me nuts. It was almost a month of relationships. I knew my best friend Roger fancied her and I figured I could maybe give her to Roger when I'm done.

'I have a feeling about you, Alvy CLEMENS. You're something special. I'd… I'd like to hold on to it.'

'Sure,' I said. 'Great.'

'What do you think about us, eh? Just the two of us being together. Going out together. Holding hands. Having a serious … you know what.'

'What?'

'Relationship!'

'Hmm… about that.'

'Say you love me? I want to hear you say it.'

I wanted to say, 'Are you fucking nuts?' but I didn't. I'm a pretty good liar, you might have noticed by now, but all her relationship talk was making me a nervous wreck. I mean, gosh. She wouldn't let go.

'Please Alvy CLEMENS? Say it.'

Hmm… saying I love you. It's not a situation that I fancy myself being in. I don't what you would've done, but me? Well, under normal circumstances I'd probably avoid eye contact and nod silently. I didn't though. I still believe I was in a nervous bipolar state or something when I grabbed the girl by her neck and screamed,

'Yeah, I love you too! I really do!'

I uttered that love you phrase as if I was reading it

out of a damn cursing book. Ha, she fell for it of

course. But that's women; born stupid, becoming stupider.

'Oh… oh Alvy CLEMENS!' she said, 'Oh Alvy.'

I really turned her on by saying it like that so

poetically and all and I recall how she squeezed my face

against her tits and how she moaned like a prostitute and

how I was just hanging in there like a clown, like Woody

Allen. It was as if she was trying to crucify me the way

she was going at it.

She really was a handful and I tell you I was so worn

out after that session we had together that I decided to

kill off the whole damn thing for good.

Yeah, so I killed off the stupid relationship. No big

personal thing trust me. I didn't phone her up and say,

'Well… girl whose name I can't remember. I… I think

it's time we should meet some new people. You know,

explore new relationships for a change. That kind of a

thing.'

I don't do that sort of thing.

I just avoided her you see. I didn't answer the phone.

I sneaked out of the house when she tried to knock the

door of my house down. I didn't show my face at the bars

she went to. She got the message eventually.

I must admit though, I felt bad about it all afterwards

because I'm not usually the one that kills off

relationships, for I don't usually enter relationships.

Maybe I should've said something to make her understand my

character. But… but what am I supposed to do when someone

starts asking personal questions out of a magazine that

some depressed old virgin lady wrote? What kind of

questions is that? And share feelings? Christ, who on

earth does that?

Maybe, maybe if I done what I said earlier by taking

her head off with a chainsaw, replacing it with one of

those girls you get in the women magazines, then I

would've tried to keep the relationship going for a while

longer because she had a terrific body.

Gosh, I don't even remember that girl's name. That's

very unimpressive I say.

Well, I guess that girl is doing fine right now, but…

but don't worry about her I tell you; she's not the going

to be the next Mark Shuttleworth or the next President.

She's not going to be the next Marie Curie or something,

trust me. She's not going to change the world if you know

what I mean. Maybe she'll get her body on a faceless

magazine one day, but that's about it. Even… even if she

gets it in there though, it'll make no difference to Alvy

CLEMENS. To tell you the truth, I despised every second

of our time together.

Chapter Eleven

Anyway, so after that stupid film school course I took and everything I told you about it, I decided not to pursue a career in the motion picture business. You see… they just didn't take me seriously as a director. All they wanted is acting, acting, acting! Dean who? Dean who?

I'd rather watch motion pictures from now on.

If there comes a time when I'm stinking rich and bored with everything in my life, then maybe I'll think about it. But when I think about it, this is not America, the land of opportunity and all.

This is Cape Town, South Africa.

All I see is a lot of poor people and a few rich people and all the poor people are working their butts off for the rich people without them getting any richer and the rich people, with all their money are just getting richer and richer. If someone can explain to me why that is, I'll try to arrange that some sort of statue be made of you or just something that'll make you feel good.

I don't want to get too sentimental about this whole rich getting richer business. Especially not on my birthday. Once you do and get preoccupied with it all, you just get depressed all over. There is only so much you can say about it because after a while you realize there's nothing you can do and that you just have to live with it.

When I was younger, I dreamt of changing the world the way I liked it to be. I don't know what happened to that dream. I used to love dreaming all kinds of things I'd wanted to do with the world, but I can't remember the last time I dreamed of anything really good. It's not even worth it nowadays. When you've made peace with yourself that your dreams won't come true, then it's easier to get through the day.

That's how I find it to be.

Hmm... maybe I can do a movie about it all when I'm rich, bored, and irritated with my no-good life. Like in that motion picture we saw at that despicable film school. What was it again? Oh, with that Orson Wells guy playing Citizen Kane and all. And his poor little Rosebud.

That movie cracked me up if you want to know the truth. Yeah, I know, Mr. Kane and Rosebud is a bit old and out of fashion for today's modern people, its human nature I suppose, but to be quite frank, I'm quite a sucker for the classical things in life.

Chapter Twelve

Everybody calls me Alvy. Everybody calls me that. It used to be a joke when I was still little, you know... being Little Alvy. But now it's just Alvy, sometimes even Alvy Crusoe CLEMENS. Gosh, they can name me after the President if it makes them happy. I don't mind. My mother says she named me after that Tom Sawyer guy. Gee, I don't know. She probably named me after a weather pattern so something.

Anyway, after the film school business and after the President and I had a nice little chat about how great life treats a person and all that, Uncle Lennie, the cheese maker who was on holiday, he came back and I nearly had a heart attack because of it. I tell you, Uncle Lennie was a real hero of mine. You see... he owned this cheese factory just outside the city which was quite brilliant. Apparently, yes apparently he was one of the best cheese makers in the country or something like that. I don't know... cheese isn't something that really excites me, but I still think that for a Brooklynite it's quite an achievement.

But that's what he did. Made cheese.

Yahoo.

Then there were his two sons, Ronnie and Joe of course. I just… just can't stand those two if you want to know. They're so phony. Always trying to sound so intellectual about everything. I think I've mentioned them before, didn't I? Yeah. Well, the less I say about them, the better.

Fortunately, Ronnie left home early so I never had the privilege to spend much time with him except when we were stupid little kids. He just got out of university and does a bit of English teaching nowadays, but he always says he wants to become some actor and would you believe it he's still jealous of the fact that I appeared in a TV commercial ahead of him. What an outright phony.

Joe, he's still a student at the university. In graduate school I think. He does some philosophy course and aspires to be a professor of some sorts. He's very clever, a real genius in fact. He… he has a girlfriend also, but don't worry, she's nothing spectacular. She suffers from obesity, but please don't tell anyone, because it's supposed to be a family secret.

Anyway, I can't really explain how it came about, where it all fell into place, but… ever since my dad died three years ago, Uncle Lennie and I got real close. Not the way homosexuals get close you know, but… but Uncle Lennie and I became good friends that I can promise you.

That was until he too got the cancer and died as well. Just a couple of months ago. The freaking cancer, I hate it. I felt really good…no… I mean I felt really bad about Uncle Lennie getting the cancer because he was a good man with strong principles. I mean, he… had good values and all. Never used prostitutes or anything I think, although he did end up marrying one. And also, he helped my mother and I a great deal after my dad died.

But my Uncle Lennie died in the hospital off all places just before Christmas and then there were all sorts of complications with his last wishes and it got real messy because I ended up nearly in court about it. All thanks to Ronnie and Joe.

Uncle Lennie even went to church, that's how great he was and not only during Christmas and all those religious days, no, he was a member, had a subscription and everything. He was very big on church I remember. He just loved the church. He was crazy about it. Obsessed completely. I tell you, it's a shame my Uncle Lennie didn't get to receive the Nobel Prize for all his religious efforts.

Actually, I despise the place. Yes, the church. But I'm
not a Satanist or anything. Don't think that. I don't
have blueprints of how to end Christianity. I believe in
Jesus, I really do. It's just that with all the rituals
and crap with the church and all, it's so phony. So
pretentious. What I mean is, Uncle Lennie, he was a
racist, but actually I'm not allowed to mention it. Very
big on the greatness of Apartheid and everything. You get
the picture of church, don't you? It's full of
pretentious fanatics.

But his visits were the best.

You see; I remember all Uncle Lennie's frequent visits
at my lousy home on weekends, I remember it like
yesterday. Uncle Lennie, he… he usually walked down
because his house was just a few blocks from ours. He had
a nice house, not that big, no house is big in this
neighborhood you know, but Uncle Lennie had a really nice
house if you know what I mean. It even had a swimming
pool.

Now… during his visits, Uncle Lennie, he'll talk to my
mother for a few minutes, just because you know… she's
family. They'll talk about things in the community, how
this old lady is doing, if that guy is still cheating on
his wife and of course; they'll talk about the weather.

Then, after all the grown-up talk, Uncle Lennie gets excused from my mother's company and search for that of Alvy CLEMENS.

My mother, well, as you can see, there isn't really much I can say about her even if I wanted to. I tell you, if she's not out doing social work helping old people who have already outlived their days on earth, she hangs around the house all day long, cleaning it twice a day while philosophizing about the weather as if the world is going to end tomorrow.

Nowadays, she just keeps on telling me to get a job, cut my hair, and to work on my speech because sometimes I talk too fast, which makes me irritated and depressed at the same time. She also wears this bloody dressing gown every day that drives me crazy. She bought it from some old gypsy woman who tells fortunes. Yeah, my mom is pretty high up in that crap too. She should've been a gypsy that crazy woman.

She's got all the qualities.

Uncle Lennie though, being in the church and all, he wasn't really worried about my mother. He knew of what a tough time she was going through with her trying to make ends meat after my dad died. Uncle Lennie lost his wife too so he knew a little about the subject. No that his

wife died also. No, his wife left him for good. The two
of them got separated, and then divorced. Ronnie and Joe
get to see that lady, but I haven't seen her for ages. It
nearly broke Uncle Lennie's spirits. I asked him a few
times about his ex-wife and all that stuff. He didn't
feel like having an intellectual discussion about it
though. You see, Uncle Lennie married a prostitute, and
she was real pretty. Unfortunately she couldn't let go of
her old habits. The story is that she, in a moment of
weakness, again got down and dirty with some unknown John.
What I don't understand is why she left Uncle Lennie. It
doesn't make any sense, does it? Nevertheless, Uncle
Lennie was very concerned of how I treated my own damn
mother.

'Listen, Alvy. I don't want to sound rude or anything,
but please, as your uncle, respect your mother even if you
don't want to. Yeah, I know she gets on you're case
sometimes, but what the heck. I lived with my parents
until I got married; I was thirty years old. Can you
imagine how that must've been for me?'

'I know, you're right,' I'd say sarcastically. 'Right
on the money there, Uncle Lennie. Well put.'

'It's not funny, Alvy. She's a good and proud woman
and she's not having it easy right now. Who'd you think

is going to take care of you when she's gone?'

'Yeah, I know,' I'd say. 'I definitely should do something about it.'

'I mean, she is your mother. And she is a good woman believe me Alvy.'

'You're right. I'll think about it.'

Good woman my ass if you ask me. I knew he wasn't serious about his damn preaching and all, but Uncle Lennie considered himself as some kind of godfather after my dad died. That's what I figured anyhow. I would quickly change the subject to things we usually talk about as quickly as possible when he started to talk serious issues.

'Say, who'd you think is going to win the rugby on Saturday?' I'll ask him.

'Hmm… let me see.   It's going to be tough I tell you, but…'

You see, whenever I mentioned sports the whole mood of conversation would change just like that and we'd talk about sports all day long. I tell you it was great having him around and I remember how I once called him dad, after my dad died of course. You know my dad, that mute I was telling you about? I don't know why I did that, calling Uncle Lennie dad, it was probably just part of my speech impediment, but Uncle Lennie; he just looked at me and smiled about it as if he knew where I was coming from. He really was like a father to me, Uncle Lennie. He really was. Even though he had a suspicion that I've been in prison for stealing and all, but he didn't say anything about my bad habits.

After all, everybody has a bad habit here and there.

Uncle Lennie's bad habit was his bad hearing, not to mention his hatred towards black people. Especially our very own President. Can you believe that? He hated Jews as well. Couldn't stand them in fact. It's a pity, because I'm not really like that you know. Still, Uncle Lennie and I were good friends and I tell you it went on for years. Of course, it helped when he gave me a few lousy bucks now and then, I tell you it helped a lot, but I liked him as a person as well. He was a very funny guy. Especially when he got drunk and I had to drag him away from the night bars all the time because he was one of those drunks that got loud and noisy. People, they don't like that nowadays.

Uncle Lennie was quite a popular guy.

A real peach.

A real socialite.

And… and with a good-looking guy like me hanging around

a popular guy, it kind a made me feel even more good-looking. Except for this Jewish nose I have. I don't know if I've mentioned, but it makes me a bit self-conscious.

Uncle Lennie never suffered from that. He always went to the night bars all by himself and by the time he got out of there, he knew every name in that bar including the barman that gave him free drinks as well as what they did for a living and all that. He also had pretty good relationships with the prostitutes there, and they all were very friendly.

Unfortunately, the pretty girls didn't really fancy him much because he wore the most horrible of clothes. I mean, even the prostitutes were scared of him. I tell you, my Uncle Lennie looked like one of those sailors at sea. He hardly shaved that bastard. I've tried hard to help him in that department because it's very important how a person looks, but the problem is… I dress exactly like that myself.

Like a bum.

But… but the thing about me is; I'm a stylish bum. A good-looking bum.

My mother, she dresses like a gypsy, but my Uncle Lennie, he dressed like a bum and it's not so much that he had bad taste, no, it was more that Uncle Lennie didn't give a damn what he had on in the morning just as long he weren't naked for the rest of his day. He just didn't bother. That was his whole philosophy on being dressed. One could say that he dressed like a bum only… only that he wasn't a bum.

Again, kind of like me.

Except at church where he wore a black suit, his only and favourite suit. I remember at my dad's funeral a couple of years ago where he also wore that black church suit and he looked pretty good in it too. So at least he dressed for special occasions.

But… but that's why Uncle Lennie didn't have any luck with women after his wife left him because of the way he dressed and looked. I've never seen him with a woman since his wife left him and I also haven't seen pursuing one either, but I don't think it bothered him much.

'Women,' my Uncle Lennie once said, 'they make fools out of everybody. Especially… especially the pretty ones.'

For me, Uncle Lennie was the Messiah from heaven, although to be quite frank, his sex life probably went to hell.

Chapter Thirteen

Uncle Lennie lived alone before he died last Christmas. Poor thing. Ronnie had long left home by then. Joe was at university. So I was about the only one who took care of him, with the cancer and all. He had a nurse who came every day to check up on him. The cancer, it's so quick you know.

First, it was just a few coughs and a couple of mild fevers, but then, only a few months after getting diagnosed, things kind a turned nasty for Uncle Lennie. In the end, that nurse took him to a hospital. That was the… how can I put, the beginning of the end for the old man. I've mentioned that my uncle was a very church going kind a guy, so I'm not that worried, you know. If what the church say is true, then my uncle… he must be in heaven right at this moment. According to the church, he's probably waving at me right now. I'm not familiar with the whole selection process of who goes to heaven and who doesn't.

Trust me I know nothing about it.

But I tell you, if my Uncle Lennie didn't made it to heaven, if that's the case, then I won't even pitch for judgment day. Like I said, I'm not a Satanist, but when

it comes to the afterlife and all that crap, I'm a
complete nutcase.

So Uncle Lennie was dying, the freaking cancer, just
like my dad. They were brothers, there you have it.
Uncle Lennie, his… his sat in the brain of all places and
the doctors reminded of its serious nature, very serious
nature. It really was a troublesome time personally that
and… and I asked Uncle Lennie before why our family are
prone to getting the cancer. He just said,

'Genes Genes. It's all in the genes, Alvy. It's what
we are made of inside that matter.'

'I'll get it too then,' I said.

'Heh? What's that?'

'I will get it too then.'

'Oh, probably,' he said, 'but you know Alvy… maybe they
will have some sort of cure for the damn thing. Just
maybe… maybe they will have. You know these clever
scientists; they're like artists nowadays. Like that
Picasso.'

Uncle Lennie was obsessed with Picasso. He really was.
He once read an autobiography on the guy and ever since
that day, he compared everything to Picasso. He was
Picasso mad. Van Gogh too.

'What has Picasso got to do with it? Wasn't he a

painter or something?'

'Nothing moves me like his <u>Weeping Woman</u>.'

'What has an artist got to do with cancer?'

'Uh?'

So for the moment I don't worry about the cancer because I know some smartass Picasso scientist will probably find a cure when I do get it eventually. That's if Uncle Lennie's right about it. But I still hate it. God, I hate the cancer. I don't mind people dying, all of us have to at some point, but I tell you, the cancer really sucks the living hell out of a person. It really does.

Gee, you know what? The cancer Uncle Lennie had was so bad, I Alvy CLEMENS saw with his own eyes how his uncle's body turned into some bony skeleton. Unbelievable I tell you. It was like looking at a… a dead corpse or something.

There at the hospital they put all kinds of machines and tubes unto his weak body like if they're going to use him as some kind of a lab experiment. Gosh, the poor guy. I really felt miserable seeing him like that. I told you I'm a pretty considerate and sensitive person, and… and seeing Uncle Lennie like that really changed me. It's kind of emotional telling you all this I tell you. I… I remember how there was this wooden chair at his bedside in the hospital, a nice comfortable chair I must admit. After a while, it became my chair for I was the daily regular visitor. I usually sat on that wooden chair, staring at dull hospital walls when Uncle Lennie was sleeping, with all the tubes and machines hanging over his face. Oh, those were the days I cried like that <u>Weeping Woman.</u> I would look at Uncle Lennie sleeping and I would try to imagine how the old man looked like when he was about my age. He must've been handsome, because his wife, I know she was real pretty and a prolific ex-prostitute. Yup, Uncle Lennie decided to marry a prostitute, but he really loved her I tell you, even… even after she left him. But he looked old at that hospital, very old I tell you. Hey, I did say that the cancer really sucks the living hell out of a person, didn't I? And when the cancer starts messing around with ones head like it did with Uncle Lennie toward the end, then that's when I really felt like pulling the plug for the old man.

You know… just to let him rest in peace.

Yup, I sat there looking at him at the hospital for a long time and when he'd woken he would look at me also and then I'd wonder if he really is looking at me or not because the cancer made him cross-eyed. But… but when his

eyes came into focus, my uncle Lennie would look me
straight in the eye and then the tears would start running
down my cheeks. And when he saw the tears running down my
cheeks, he would take my hand and squeeze it as hard as he
could with his skeleton hands and then the tears would
really start running down my cheeks.

'People ought to die, Alvy CLEMENS,' Uncle Lennie told
me on his deathbed with a dying voice. 'They way of life
they say.'

'But… I don't…'

'And it's the duty of those left behind to mourn the
dead.'

'Who said that?'

'It doesn't matter?'

'Was it Picasso?'

'Yes. It was Picasso.'

I remember lots of crying that day.

'You mourn me, Alvy CLEMENS!' Uncle Lennie yelled.
'You mourn the hell out of me!'

I didn't look in his eyes again after those stupid
moments of crying we had together. I got too emotional.

But… but at his funeral, I cried like a madman. I'm
not a crybaby you know, don't even think that, but the
guy's my uncle. And a great one. Gee, he wanted to be

mourned. He asked me to and… and you know what? It made
me feel better. Just about everything.

Anyway, Uncle Lennie was my very own Messiah. Ronnie
and Joe, his own flesh and blood, they didn't give a damn
about him and his last wishes. Not a damn I tell you.
Even at the funeral I remember, the two of them sat there
looking like statues while I… I was crying like a damn
child. I really don't feel like discussing it, but… but
let me just say that Ronnie and Joe, his two sons, let me
just say that they didn't make anyone proud for what they
did.

Apparently, Uncle Lennie wanted me to be a part of his
last wishes and so we had this half-hour court case and it
got messy. Now I'm not a part of Uncle Lennie's will but
I'd rather not discuss what happened at that damn court
case.

Regarding the will, I think I've said it all along and…
and if I didn't, then I'm saying it now: Money, it's not
that important to me. It really isn't you know. Yeah…
I'd say that I didn't care so much for Uncle Lennie's
money like I'm making it out to be.

Uncle Lennie, now he was a very clever and sensible
guy. Very down to earth if you what I mean. I really
miss him. I still miss him sometimes. Apart from my

mother and my best friend Roger, Uncle Lennie was the only person that remembered my birthday every single time. Joe and Ronnie, you know those two? Haven't heard a anything from them today. Not a thing.

You want to know what Uncle Lennie gave me last Christmas? A .45 revolver. Yup, it's very special.

'Here you go Alvy. Merry Christmas.'

'What's this?'

'It's a damn gun. A .45. I don't need it anyway. Got plenty.'

'Mine?'

'Us whites have to protect ourselves you know. You know, from the blacks.'

'Gee, thanks.'

'Merry Christmas.'

'What… what should I do with it?'

'Practice. Get it licensed first.'

'Thanks.'

'I'm… I'm not saying you should go and shoot somebody you know, like eh… let's say… the President. Just… just keep it and who knows, maybe it comes in handy.'

'Whoa, thanks again.'

'Maybe it will come in handy Alvy.'

It's a real beauty I tell you. I've got it licensed
and everything. It's black and Uncle Lennie even got my
name engraved on it. ALVY CLEMENS in capitals. It's my
most valuable possession I tell you. It really is.
Usually what I do is… is that I go and shoot rats at the
petrol factory across the highway nearby where I live.
You know, just for the hell of it.

It's great.

Letting go of all the frustrations and everything.

My mom gave me shampoo for my birthday today. Last
year I got a pair of socks from her. Gosh, next year I'll
probably get a bar of soap. Just great. And it's not as
if we are poor like hell. We can afford birthday presents
you know. It's just that my mom, she loves me I know, but
she doesn't think anymore. She's like a parrot, talking
about the weather all day long and talking about my days
as a TV commercial star. As if that's the only things of
things to talk about.

Listen, if Uncle Lennie was to be still alive right now, I
definitely wouldn't be sitting here having a good old
birthday bash all alone while telling you about everything
that went wrong in my life. I wouldn't. Uncle Lennie,
that old man, he wouldn't have allowed it. Never.

Chapter Fourteen

Well, being it my birthday and all, I guess I should stop rambling on and on about how I messed up all the great opportunities that was handed to me on a silver platter. Nothing really to write home about as you can see. When I think of it now, maybe I should've settled starring in TV commercials, make good money and keep my mouth shut. Maybe I should've accepted a normal job like everybody else and work my ass off. Be a regular citizen just like everybody else.

But oh no, Alvy CLEMENS wanted to be different. He didn't want to be stuck into some lousy routine work for the rest of his life like so many others. Alvy wanted to be different.

Don't get me wrong, I want to be famous, I really want to. It's just that, I don't know… in some crazy way I feel I can make a difference, change the world if you can call it.

Some lousy friend told me the other day that happy is the man who can make a living through his hobby. He said he read it somewhere but hell… I don't know…

Yes, I have plans, big plans I tell you. But somehow… somehow I struggle to get my plans into action because I

don't seem able to get a break from this crazy world we
live in.

Anyway, as I said before, I don't think my nephews Ronnie
and Joe felt anything serious for Uncle Lennie, his own
flesh and blood. I really don't think so. And... you know
what? I don't think they give a damn about me either.
It's my birthday today, right? Haven't heard a thing from
those two today. Not a thing. You see what I'm dealing
with here, eh? My best friend, Roger, he phoned me all
the way from Paris yesterday just to congratulate me. It
must've cost the poor guy a fortune, but he still... he
still phoned me and made me feel good. Now that's what I
call friendship.

   Roger and I had this silly old fight before he left for
Paris last Christmas and on top of that Uncle Lennie died
suddenly. Uncle Lennie supposedly would've given me the
money to go overseas, just so that I can go along with
Roger. The rest, well, the rest is history. Ronnie and
Joe are probably laughing their asses off; that's how
insensitive they are about these things. Uncle Lennie, he
thought it was a great idea and he really supported me on
it all. Traveling the world as a bum and everything. We
talked about it for weeks I remember.

What a great guy.

My mother really wanted me to go overseas you know.
She still wants me to go can you believe it. Even more
now with her and Michael K. becoming intimate and all.

'It's about time you leave the house and take care of
yourself for a change,' she keeps on saying.

'It's my house too,' I'll keep on telling her.

'Yes, but Michael and I, we need a bit of quality time
alone. No use you crawling up on us all the time, Alvy.
Just no use.'

Yeah right. Crawl up on them when they're busy
screwing in the living room. Crawling up on them my ass.

Yahoo.

I tell you, I don't what it is; love or lust, but
those two just can't keep their hands of each other.

'No use you crawling up on us all the time, Alvy. No
use.'

'How can I crawl into the living room?'

'Don't start now, Alvy CLEMENS. Don't start with me
now. I think you know what Michael and I mean.'

It means that my mother and that boyfriend Michael K.
sneaks around the house like little children just so that
I won't have to see them do their… you know their primal
duties and that… that's probably the main reason why she

wanted me out of the house and still wants me out of the house, due to me disturbing the peace between her and that boyfriend Michael K. from bringing down the house because of they're all day going at it. The only time she doesn't yell or have a heart attack about the television or the stereo being too loud is when she's at it with Michael K. in her bedroom because then she thinks I won't hear them moaning and groaning, but those two are at it like pigs if you ask me.

Real squealing pigs.

However, that's nothing compared to what my mother was like when I was still a little kid and when she was still crucifying my dad. They were going at it in the living room, bedroom, bathroom, even in the garden. I saw them a few times going at it and that's why I say that mother loved dad a lot.

My dad, he was a mute sure enough, but I tell you he was an animal in bed. It was like watching one of these nature programs on television where the male sea lions go after the female sea lions. Have you ever seen those things go at it, eh, have you? Well, I tell you, my mom and dad, they were like freaking sea lions in their younger days. That's probably the reason why I've got such a sexual personality, because of all the sexual energy I experienced during my childhood and all.

I remember having my first orgasm in the fourth grade.

But those two, my mother and that boyfriend Michael K., they want me to go overseas just so that they can get some privacy, but… but like I said, I hardly see them go at it like my mom and dad used to go at it. They're not like sea lions, but more like a couple of excited monkeys if you know what I mean. Nah, there's not anything special about the way they go at it. Nothing at all.

Chapter Fifteen

Anyway, this guy I told you about just now that I wanted
to go overseas with, my friend Roger, he and I had this
silly fight over a damn dog, my dog, and off he went
overseas with some prostitute. I don't think I would've
gone with him in any case though. He was a messed up
addict, whilst I… I wanted to travel and see the world on
my own, like that Hemingway character. I didn't want to
work myself to pieces in some bloody Paris restaurant like
that Roger was going to do. I'm an adventurer, like
Robinson Crusoe.

   Still, that Roger had some confidence I tell you. In
himself that is. He should've been a comedian or
something and… and if it weren't for the day of the big
fight we had because of my dog that died and where I had
to beat the crap out him because I wanted to mourn and pay
my damn respects to the dog, we still would've been the
best of friends.

   Who knows? I probably would've gone with him to work
in the stinking restaurants and factories as well. I miss
the guy you know. Especially on my birthday. He was such
an interesting character, with his funny red hair and big
glasses. He just looked so funny. But… but a compulsive

liar! I swear, not even a lie detector would detect him.
Roger I mean. He loves it. It's his hobby. A gift from
above.

I remember this one time, we were sitting at some nasty
looking Brooklyn bar late at night and there were drunks
and prostitutes lying all over the place. It was very
late and I was tired, and… and I saw Roger with some
addict and I waited for him at some lousy table, ready to
go home. I… I remember some decent old guy with his wife
joining me and he started telling me chapters about the
brilliance of fishing and the difficulty getting that big
fish. I was rather enjoying the conversation because it
was rather stimulating. I was also getting sober with the
old man talking fishing all the time. I tell you, that
old man had some real wisdom with his fishing chapters.
He looked pretty educated on top of it too.

Anyway, Roger interrupted in comic fashion, looking
like that Woody Allen, with his slimy red hair and
glasses, trying to attract the couple's attention of how
wonderful great and funny he is. He muttered like a damn
child,

'Hmm… hmm… the first prostitute I met was right here
in this place.' The old man turned his face away from me

and looked at Roger in earnest. I closed my eyes
pretending to be Hemingway at sea.

'Where, here?'

'Right here…,' said Roger scratching his baby chin.
'Right here where you're sitting I'm sure I met that good
prostitute. Uh-uh.'

'That must've been fond memories,' said the wise old
man and laughed together with his wife.

'Christ, I was sitting right here next to Alvy when she
flung herself on that chair where you're sitting. I could
see in her eyes she wanted to fuck me but her eyes were
also tired and sad. So I bought her lunch instead.'

'That sounds rather polite.'

'But listen, I bought her lunch and I made jokes and
she started smiling and I felt all worked up and all.
When we finished I took her back to my place and I fucked
her for free. Ha!'

What a terrible joke! The old man didn't take it that
funny either.

'Uh, why did you do that?'

'Well, it was a good opportunity and I took it. Thanks
for asking.'

'But you said she's a…'

'She's a woman who wanted a good time.'

The old man didn't ask any further questions and Roger looked at him very superior like. I Alvy CLEMENS was just sitting there half-drunk with dark moods and all.

'Like I said, she was the first prostitute I met here in this bar. Since then I had many. Didn't know the first thing about Pauline.'

'Who's Pauline?'

'Oh, that's my girlfriend. But she's in Paris now doing films and stuff and I'm really crazy about her.'

'Is that so?' asked the old man, trying to understand this Roger character.

'Sure, she wants to get married and all and have children.'

'But that's really terrific.'

'But she cheated on me with one of my good friends from school. And then… then slept with his father. To me that was a bit over the top, so… so I decided to end the relationship. But oh, she's still the only girl for me.'

'But you said you had a girlfriend…'

'I did, but Pauline also has a sister. She's in Paris too I've heard. Gee, they're twins, same and all.'

'Are you a nutter, boy?'

'In fact old man, eh… at that time I was still seeing Tania, although June didn't like her first thing. Said

the whore had gnohorrea, but how was I to know, and June
wanted my children real bad. Your old head still
following, eh?'

    'Who the hell is June?'

    'Oh, that's my wife.'

    'Christ, son. Take it easy.'

    'Yeah… well… Alvy got into Tania too, but he threw a
lot of money at her during his acting days. You remember
that Tania girl, eh Alvy? She… she told me she's kind of
selective, but I guess the whole money thing and Alvy
being all famous blew her over. So I was pretty much
asexual during that time because… because see old man;
unlike these whores I prize fidelity, and I couldn't find
a girl I could really trust. I'm very big on trust and in
the end I couldn't trust anyone. Gosh, so I tried to jump
off Table Mountain instead. What's worse, it took me half
a day to climb the mountain in the first place…'

    'Eh… slow down son. What are we talking about here?'

    'Christ old man. It was supposed to be a damn picnic
on that mountain! Hey Alvy, you remember, eh? But our
friend Scott got lost when we started drinking, near base
camp I suppose. When we came back he was lying half-naked
under a tree, mugged by a couple of Russian immigrants who
earlier assaulted a lesbian couple near the top for a

drunken reason. It was hot like hell that day and those
Russians had it bad.   They even stuffed some book up way
deep inside Scott's rectum, one hell of a book, Anna
Karenina or something.   And gee… that Alvy madman you're
sitting next to, eh, he was nuts I remember, chasing after
a baboon with sharpened sticks and whisky, looking like a
no-good. I remember he came back with blood on his hands,
smiling and cursing at the same time, holding a dead
rabbit. Yahoo. We… we were so stuffed after that picnic
with the dead rabbit we went straight back home, but gosh,
I still would like to jump off Table Mountain one day you
know. '

The old man and his wife shook their heads in disbelief,
with the old man saying 'Uh… excuse me fellows,' and left
right there and Roger looked at me astonished and made
some realistic donkey sounds that were irritating like
hell. But… but the old man didn't respond to Alvy's
antics. He just left with that ex-prostitute of his.

   I tell you, that Roger lie detector lied about
absolutely everything; about his parents, how much money
he had, how much drugs he used and abused, how he was
involved in a Colombian drug bust, how his dad worked at a
Jackie Chan picture set, about his lousy sex life, he even

lied to me about his first name, his own damn Christian
name I tell you.

   He also lied about those stinking factories and
restaurants overseas where he told me that once I've
finished working there I wouldn't have to work again for
the rest of my life. What a peach of a lie. I tell you,
he lied so often that after a while I had to stop myself
falling from my freaking chair every time he was going on
about something because it was just so funny listening to
the guy. His lies were just so hard to believe it gets
ridiculous to be honest. It's not even depressing
listening to him. He's just a nutcase, a complete
nutcase. He really belongs in therapy. I'm not joking.
Gosh, I wish you were there to see this guy with his funny
red hair and big glasses. A clown. You really should've
seen him trying to impress everyone about his
achievements. I'm a kleptomaniac I swear, but Roger, that
guy is a compulsive liar. He must've grown up alongside a
lie detector or something.

   It's just… the whole drug thing messed him up you know.
I still figure him to be worthless because of it.

Roger was intelligent though and very smart. He was a
writer sometimes who crapped out some pretty good and

interesting stories when sober. He was a real Hemingway nutcase, and also into that Fitzgerald drunk, who apparently had a crazy wife. Roger hinted on some book he was working on and I remember reading it once or twice, but he never got further than page ten or so that Roger. It's very depressing how he writes but he really is a terrific writer I think. I mean his book eh… *Zelda - wife of Scott, enemy of Ernest* had real potential. I mean… take a look at these rough pages:

There was a time when I was sick and mad and I wanted to die but I met a girl who made me happy for a while and I thought she could make me happy for good. She was young and care-free and made me feel better and I wanted to get married and spend the rest of my life with her but she was also mad and I found out only after I fell in love and I felt guilty. So I kept on loving her despite and she broke my heart but I didn't care because I felt to have her. I don't know why but I felt so lonely I wanted to die so I took her back and we both were miserable and got drunk often and we were fools. She was miserable and tried to kill herself and I hated her for doing that but I kept on loving her because I was lonely like hell and didn't want anyone else that I can make miserable too. I

felt worthless being so miserable and I blamed her for
everything, but she kept on trying to kill herself and I
tried too but I'm worthless and couldn't do it so I tried
to kill Zelda instead for she was pretty and young and
care-free. I tried to kill you too and I failed in that
too. Forgive me.

Congrats on your book. We all here loved it. Say hi to
Pauline.
Your most handsome Scott

Roger was possessed in his writing, and was always busy on
that book of his. I have a few pages of it now in front
of me and there's some good stuff in here. Gosh, it was
either Scott Fitzgerald or Ernest Hemingway. Roger was
obsessed by those two. Look how descriptive and all he
gets here with old Hemingway in this diary crap of Scott:

Paris 1924
He is everything they told me about. His eyes are that of
a brilliant man and he was a brilliant conversationalist.
We talked literature all day long and he's so passionate
about the book he's busy writing, as well as the books he
still wants to write. Everything he does it seems is

geared for writing his books. I have never met someone so

determined. He is indeed the real thing.

                    *   *   *

I didn't impress Ernest much. I got drunk pretty quickly

and he dismissed me for that and he laughed and ridiculed

me in front his cross-eyed friends who knew nothing about

literature. I dragged myself away home and Zelda was

missing but I was drunk. I really thought Ernest would

take to me from the beginning because I'm a famous writer

and he's a drunk. He looks strong and impressive and

could beat the hell out of anyone on his day. I haven't

met any of his literary friends but he agreed to meet me

again the following day. And so we did meet and we didn't

drink and I gave him This Side Of Paradise to read and he

told me afterwards he almost got a haemorrhage reading it.

The bastard loved it!

I tell you, I always felt Roger being a good writer and

all. I mean, he's got a distinct kind of voice when it

comes to literature. And that's why the guy went to Paris

in the first place, to get into character and all for the

book he obsesses over. But poor Roger. He really is a

wretched person when it comes to drugs and alcohol. Paris
is full of that too I hear. And Roger, well, people
rarely change you know.

   Look, I'm a pretty considerate person and I don't want
to run addicts like Roger down like I don't want to run
girls who aren't so good-looking down either, but some
things will never change. I tell you, they'll never come
right, those addicts. Maybe here and there one lucky
addict will make it unbelievably and that addict really
should get a statue made of him, an… an odorless statue of
course, so that a hundred years from now everyone will
remember him for what a great guy he has become. I
experimented with drugs when I was younger because I
wanted to know why everyone, including Roger, was making
such a big fuss about it.

   But drugs, drugs are not for me. I like being a crook
or a kleptomaniac once in a while because it makes me feel
as if I'm alive again, but… but doing drugs? Waste of
time I tell you.

   The way I see it, the main reason why people use those
filthy chemicals is that they refuse to accept the fact
that life isn't such a wonderful and satisfying experience
their parents once told them it was going to be. But
that's the thing about parents.

Always wrong about everything.

And they remind me of lecturers.

It's funny you know. Roger was one friend besides dead Uncle Lennie who remembers my birthday every time. And you won't believe this, but yesterday afternoon, the son of a bitch phoned me all the way from Paris to congratulate me on my birthday. I'm not kidding. I don't even remember when Roger was born, I promise you. That tells you something. Maybe I'm the son of a bitch around here and not him. I really should call him up and ask him out for a beer or something like that when he comes back so that we can talk about Paris and all that.

Chapter Sixteen

I always wanted to go to the countryside so I could see the cows, the pigs and the big farms with all the country fresh air. That would be great, really terrific. But it's so enormously big there in the countryside and everyone look at me so funny you know. It's scary. Not only because of all the funny looks I get, but when I go outside the city and into the countryside I get so nervous because I'm afraid that I'll get bit by a spider or a poisonous snake and then I fear that no countryside medicine would be able to cure me. It's a different world out there you know.

I tell you now though… if I'm to born again in another lifetime different from this one you know, I want it to be on a farm where I can learn to take care of myself and not depend on other people so much. I'm not kidding.

I'll make my own milk.

I'll grow my own fruit.

I'll have my own meat, meat from cattle, meat from sheep, meat from pigs, meat from horses, meat from anything that has flesh in it and that tastes good.

I'll do everything on my own because once you depend on other people too much you get lost somewhere along the line. It's true.

That's why I wanted to get married and make babies with
this girl, eh… Helen… Helen Koransky and she had some
money and I thought that maybe we can settle being a
married couple and all in the countryside. I figured
Helen could've supported me financially too. She was a
psychiatrist, or trying to become one I should say. A
real beauty, very decent and everything. She also
mentioned that she's from an important family and all.

   I… I still think of her as the girl of my dreams
because she was everything that a guy like me wants in a
girl, with regards to looks, money and personality; you
know, all the good stuff good-looking guys like me care
about. She was a very decent girl and had big breasts and
I remember being very fond of them. She was a real
countryside girl. Built like a stallion, but hmm… let me
see… brunette, fair skin, longish prostitute legs, decent
face… she was a good one. She… she was the only girl I
can honestly say that I fantasized about constantly
without actually becoming too intimate and all.

   Maybe it's also because she looked so innocent about
everything, as if she figured that when I stared at her
breasts I was actually staring at something else. But I

tell you, I was staring at those breasts in a very big
way!

She… she wanted to be a psychiatrist and she knew
everything about that Freud guy, from his whole damn
childhood, his cocaine addiction, up to his crazy sex
theories. Helen was intelligent and smart, but she also
did some prostitution work you know… something I really
didn't felt comfortable with at that time. Yeah, she
successfully managed to prostitute herself through
university, paying rent and tuition. I have lots of
respect for her, because it's a tough business and many I
know fails to deal with the abuse that comes with it. It
kills them in the end. Only a select few make it work I
guess and Helen… she… she did good. There was this one
eh… Sasha I think. She tried to commit suicide seconds
after I've been with her. I never saw her after that.

Helen was very ambitious with her whole psychiatry
thing. I remember that she kept on analyzing me during
our time together. Boy, that's all she ever did with me.
We just kept on talking about our feelings and everything
you know… all those personal stuff that I was critical
about earlier and talking personal with decent girls I
tell you again… it's not that easy.

I even talked to her about the whole Kennedy

assassination and all, how it interested me and how I deeply I felt towards it. She was real pretty so that helped I guess. I tell you… I told her a lot about my personal life. About my Jewish nose, about my habit of stealing things and going to prison. Of course, I told her of how I met the President and my days as a TV star. That I told her first. Just to impress her you know. I also told her about the so-called chemical imbalance in my brain. I remember she was fascinated about it. I guess she gave me free psychiatric help by trying to explain my dreams and nightmares as if there was a meaning to it all. Especially my sex dreams. I don't think I've told you, but I have weird sex dreams at night. It's crazy because all… all of my dreams have got to do with sex to be honest. But hear, what's so strange about my sex dreams is that somehow my parents get involved in them. Weird I tell you.

Helen Koransky said it got all to do with what that Freud guy said. She kept on telling me this story, some Greek story, about this boy who kills his father because he's scared that his father might remove his testicles and… and the reason why the father wants to do the castrating thing is because he's jealous of the boy and his mother getting too close and all and eventually the boy, not knowing who his mother really was, still goes on to marry his own mother.

Something like that. Yeah, I know it sounds peachy, but what do you expect from the Greeks, eh? They're mental, every single one of them. That damn university psychiatrist was right all along.

Helen Koransky said that the bad relationship I had with my father has something to do with my sex dreams, that he being a damn mute and all dissatisfied me during my childhood. I suppose she had a point. My father was dissatisfying as hell. I never felt a damn about him. Not a damn.

Anyway, this Helen Koransky, she was very knowledgeable on sex. She knew a lot on the subject and I figure her time spent as a prostitute had its benefits. She told me there's nothing she hasn't done and she's actually more of the romantic type. She always went on about that Romeo & Juliet and all. I remember how she went on talking to me about Romeo & Juliet for hours and that the love she wants must be something like that, something deep and meaningful, like a great work of art she said.

'Like a great work of art?' I asked. 'You must explain that.'

'You see Alvy… it must be flawless, pure, like a

magnificent Renaissance painting or… or a beautifully written prose and poetry. That's how love ought to be, that's… that's how people should love each other. It should be aesthetically perfect. You see now, Alvy CLEMENS?'

'Life is not a work of art,' I told her straight away. 'Definitely not. What is art anyway? Bunch of stupid paintings. Fake imitations of life. Life is not a work of art, Helen Koransky.'

'Not life! Love… love should be art.'

'What did I say?'

'Arggh, never mind Alvy CLEMENS.'

I tell you, Helen and I had our difficult moments but gosh, what a terrific woman still. If what they say about love is true, then Helen's my girl. Not that many people I know believe in love and romance and its beauty and all that. I mean, you need a real decent heart to believe in that junk, because at the end of the day you need to make room for the sex. It's that simple.

That's why I say that romance in general gives me the creeps. It isn't something I go on about much. We used to read Shakespeare a lot at school and he didn't make much sense to me back then as he doesn't make much sense to me now.

I remember how Helen Koransky walked around with her William Shakespeare books like a lunatic and how she read all that poetry crap to herself. I swear she didn't understand a single line what that guy wanted to say, but boy… boy did she try. Poor Helen Koransky.

Helen Koransky talked about marriage, having kids; you know… all those grown-up things. A bloody romantic. Girls love that romantic crap I hear, so I tried my hand at that subject a few times. We made love many times also, but I still had to pay her for the service, which to me is rather disappointing considering how much effort I had put into the relationship. But… but she did say that she didn't want me as her lover, for she fancies girls more than she fancies men. I don't blame her for her choice you know, considering her time spent going down and dirty. If there is something I regret in life then it's definitely Helen Koransky. She was the perfect woman. Even Roger agreed with me on that point. And that guy is nuts.

Gosh, I did try, I really did. I even wrote her a poem at one of our therapy sessions in trying to impress her of my character.

'What do you think, eh? Look… at this line

seeing that she, my heart's best treasure was no more.'

'Oh, Alvy!' she said.   'That's so sweet, so romantic.

It's lovely.'

'Well, that's me,' I told her, proudly, 'a romantic.'

'Where do you come up with these stuff?'

'Eh, I don't…'

'I never knew you like poetry, Alvy? Tell me, who's

your favourite poet?'

'Eh… Shakespeare is nice. He knows how to say it… you

know. And, let me see…'

Poetry? Is it a subject?

'I guess… I guess Tom Sawyer also had some poetry in

him, you know.'

Gosh, I hate books! And poetry? What's that?

'Tom Sawyer?'

'Sure, he's deep, kind of peachy if you know what I

mean. Especially when he and Huck were philosophizing

about life and all.'

Yahoo.

Chapter Seventeen

Helen Koransky got her psychiatric degree and went off overseas to gain experience in her quest to become a women psychiatrist. I will not see her again and yeah, it was hard letting go and I guess she's probably a lesbian something after all and I guess she can kiss my ass. That's feminists for you. But still, I really liked her at some stage. Not only liked, but I kind of liked talking to her too. I may not be an expert on that pervert Freud and his crazy sex theories, but I really enjoyed talking to an intellectual and everything. It's odd, because I hate talking to girls. They make me a little nervous. Especially these clever feminists one gets nowadays.

I still fantasize about her. To tell you the truth, I love fantasizing about Helen Koransky. Not only because she being an old-fashioned prostitute, for I kind of like prostitutes in general. No, she's a good girl and still the great love of my life, that Helen Koransky. Hey, did you know that Uncle Lennie married a swinger girl? Yeah, he fell in love with her and decided to give her a chance. I only found out after, it was supposed to be a big family secret, but my mother blurted it all out in one of her bipolar/schizophrenic states. The marriage was a big success while it lasted. Poor Ronnie and Joe have got no clue. I figure they never will. Their intellectual brains wouldn't be able to quite understand how it could've occurred. I figure that those two are too gifted to understand.

But you know… they say that prostitutes make the best wives. They tend to be faithful and they know a lot about sex. When you're occupied and all, like most good-looking guys are, that's about all one can handle.

Chapter Eighteen

You know… I don't know what's wrong with me, but somehow or another I keep on picking the wrong kind of girls. Or somehow they pick me, I can't tell. Just when I think I'm beginning to get into some form of 'relationship', for no reason, I start to run like hell. Or it's the other way around. It's probably the freaking bipolar. Or, maybe I have a curse or something? Maybe there's a scar on my forehead and I haven't noticed it yet. Maybe I'm a homosexual and I haven't figured it out yet. Yeah, that's it. I'm a homosexual.

Sometimes, late at night when I'm sexually frustrated, I go and shoot rats at that petroleum factory I told you about earlier on in the day. You see I have this .45-licensed revolver that my Uncle Lennie gave me, but I told you that as well. Dammit, I really really love that revolver.

You want to know the truth? Shooting those rats with that revolver of mine? Letting go of all those frustrations I have and everything? It's better than going into damn therapy and discussing the art of staying alive. Much better I tell you.

Chapter Nineteen

And so… I got a terrific job a few weeks ago.   Nothing
spectacular.   Definitely won't change my life you know.
All I do is… is that I get a truck from this company that
tells me to drive from one place to another, deliver
packages and crap for a few lousy bucks.   What's in the
packages?   Gee, I don't even know, because the company is
pretty tight-lipped about it all.   That's how lousy the
work is.   I don't use brainpower doing it you know.   You
won't see a rocket scientist applying for this job.   You
won't see Mark Shuttleworth around here.   Definitely not
him.   Nor the President.   Nor Shakespeare.

But still… it's pretty hard work I tell you.   It really
is.   Very repetitive too you know.   Very.   Funny enough,
I… I kind of enjoy it.   Don't ask me why, please don't,
but I don't feel any pressures or anything applying my
mind to this kind of job.

I don't think so much nowadays.

Maybe that's it.   Just keep on working.   Let the
bipolar brain sort out its chemical imbalances.   Who
knows, maybe this is what I was born to do.   None of those
other things I did gave me much excitement in any case.
It was a real bore to be honest.

Hmm… I'm so sorry, but I don't really enjoy my lousy job. It was a joke. A bipolar joke. To tell you the truth, I hate my job. Boy, it's completely worthless. Going to work six days a week and saving money for a used car or a pair of nice shoes? All this while wondering if tomorrow is going to be a rainy day or if it's going to be a sunny day? Gosh, I hate it.

Today, I fall down in front of the couch after a hard day's work and I watch TV, only that I don't watch TV, I just stare at it because that's what I'm supposed to do before I fall asleep.

Today I'll meet a nice girl, but tomorrow I won't even recognize her face.

Today I'm too lazy and tired to make my own food so I eat junk food in the mornings, day and night and… while doing that, I think back to Uncle Lennie and of how I missed going out with him to the crappy bars we often went to.

Today I'm happy, tomorrow I'll be depressed again.

That's how it goes. I don't want to sound so cynical about everything. I'm just trying to make a point about my work. It gets depressing after a while. And… when I get depressed, I get this funny feeling that somebody is

watching me. Not 'You Know Who', no, something else. I
get this funny feeling that this is not real. I start
wondering to myself if it all really happened, if
everything in my life really did occur, if all my family
and friends weren't just some sort of charade, that they
along with my so-called dead uncle and father were just
great actors in some sort of motion picture.

A motion picture where I get to be the star of
character and... of how the audience gets to see every
little thing I do, of how I jerk off during the day, of
how... how I keep looking at myself in the mirror every damn
second of my life, and of... of how I pop my zits in front
of it and of how I read Huckleberry Finn while sitting on
the toilet, all that little things we don't tell each
other.

I tell you, if it wasn't for that Freud smartass and
all his crazy theories, I wouldn't even have bothered
telling you all this. I just wouldn't have bothered. You
live and you die. Isn't that's how it supposed to be?
Nowadays, everyone and I mean everyone, is going into
therapy and all to find out why they're so mental. It's
insane. Once we start questioning happiness, that's when
the problems come into being. Trust me.

But thanks Mr. Freud. You're sex interpretations are

much more interesting than my stash of pornographic

magazines. Much more.

Chapter Twenty

Do you know what a perfect world would be like for a messy guy like me?

I'll tell you.

Where everybody speaks, where everybody say what they really think about how they feel and all. If… if people can just start talking about how they really feel about somebody else or about what they really think of this crazy world we live in, I tell you, half of all our problems would be solved.

Where everybody speaks.

But unfortunately, very unfortunate I say, and this is the sad reality of living a silly life, people don't do that sort of thing. Hell, they don't even have anything to say that is worth saying. Gee, I don't know, maybe it's the President's fault. That's right.

Blame the President.

What's… what's so philosophical about that?

Anyway, even if I do have something to say on life, you pretty much heard it already in any case. (I did mention this in my introduction, so take it easy.)

Nothing spectacular.

Nothing life changing.

But, I'd like to think you know… that… that in some bizarre circumstance, my thoughts can make some difference, even if all those important philosophers will never get the chance to hear what a low-life like me has to tell about life and all. You see… all these important philosophers and academics? They live their life surrounded by books, books, and more stupid books. Yet, those same so-called people I'm mentioning are supposed to know and teach us everything that there is to teach about how we should live our lives.

Hey, I never went to Oxford or some intellectual university. I admit that it's hard putting all my thoughts and ideas into one clear and concise sentence whilst not sounding like an idiot at the same time. I sincerely apologize for the inconvenience.

But maybe you know… maybe the fact that I'm not philosophically educated makes my ideas relevant after all. You see, I'm not one of those philosophers you get that sits in a room all day long trying to figure out what life is all about. I'm not here to give you a lecture if whether life is worth living or worth dying and I'm also not telling you to go fuck yourself. You know how much I hate lectures.

I don't do that sort of thing. I figure that if all
the important philosophers talk about the same damn
issues, then there's no point for me in doing what they
are doing. Getting the picture?

What I do is that I try to see something that interest
me and then I'll focus and talk about what I just saw.
Sometimes I see something that I don't like and then I'll
talk about it even more because then there's more to talk
about because… because I feel a dislike is rather
problematic and all. But… if it happens to be that I see
something that I really like, well, then I figure it's no
use talking about it because… because it's not
problematic. I know it sounds a bit silly to you, but to
tell you the truth, life is just too short to talk about
all the good things in life. If we would go around all
day long, talking about how great everything is and how
life is just too good to be true, then it gets too boring
to be honest.

Gosh, I'm depressing.

That's why love stories that end up sad and tragic is
usually much more interesting than love stories that end
up happy and everything. I mean… look at that Shakespeare
nutcase.

I told you before that I don't like going on about

Shakespeare too much because it doesn't really interest me, but… but I still think that if people keep talking about something that happened centuries ago, then… then you should take notice of it and that's why I say that even if Shakespeare had a broken heart of a life; it must've been an interesting experience for the guy. So he had a tough time of having a broken heart all the time, but today we can safely say that Shakespeare was an interesting character that led an interesting life.

If you understand where I'm coming from, then you'll have an idea of what I'm trying to point out. I also had a pretty tough time of it, a lot of things didn't work out for me also and I still feel bad about it, but if those bad things didn't happen, I wouldn't be here talking about it. I just wouldn't have anything to say that is worth saying.

If everything worked out perfect, if my whole life turned out be one great holiday, then I'd go so far to say that I had a real bore of a life.

The way I see it, the more things turn out bad and ugly, the better you turn out in the end. Especially for a so-called manic-depressive. I used to go to prison occasionally and I tell you, I learned more about myself in that stinking place than in this so-called free place we live in. No question.

So my point is this: if you already planned to live the dream life, the life where everything turns out perfect in the end, I tell you, you're going to make a fool out of yourself because no one is going to remember you the day after your funeral. They will try to remember you, because you know… you were a good person and all, but, you lived a boring life and people tend to forget boring lives. I'm not joking.

My dad, he died of cancer when I was eighteen years old. He was a good man, but I can't remember the son of a bitch because he had no personality. He was a mute and a rather worthless character. All I remember about my dad was that he worked his ass off at some construction yard to take care of my mother and that's my dad in a nutshell. Yeah, he took care of my mother and me but why is it that I don't remember him, eh? I don't remember him making me proud or anything. Maybe he did once or twice, but like I said, I don't even remember the bastard. Nowadays, I don't even know how my dad even looked like. That, I think, tells you something.

My mother on the other hand, although she drives me mad sometimes, I'll never forget that whining old gypsy of a woman even if I wanted to. Even if she dies tomorrow, the

day after my twenty-first birthday, I still won't be able
to forget her and I don't think anyone here in Brooklyn
will forget her either, because she's the person that they
gossip about the most of in any case. My mother doesn't
even have anyone decent to talk to in our neighborhood,
except when she's out doing her crazy social work or when
she's with that rocket scientist of a boyfriend Michael
K., but my mother's got energy, she's alive, and she does
tend to lighten people's spirits.

You know what? I… I know for a fact that the day after
my mother's funeral, all of us will start to miss her even
though we didn't like her that much.

    We won't miss being with her, hell no.

    We won't miss her delightful conversations of the damn
weather.

    And global warming.

    We won't miss her talking about how great it is to be a
social worker.

    We won't miss her wearing that ugly dressing gown that
she bought off some old gypsy woman.

    Nothing of that.

    It's just that without my dear mother, there won't be
anything funny to talk about anymore. And… and if we

can't talk to each other and if we can't make each other
laugh, we might as well end up getting drunk.

Which brings us to Alvy CLEMENS, the real hero of this
picture.

I was a bit unlucky to be honest. I really was. Luck,
what a silly word that is, eh? Probably the silliest word
ever invented. Every time I hear of this and that foolish
character who just won the national lottery, I just feel
like breaking my leg or something. I really do you know.
I don't know if you've noticed, but winners of lotteries
always promise that half of their winnings will be donated
to some AIDS orphanage or that they're going to open up a
school for blind people. It's crazy. Why do they have
to lie their socks off if they don't feel like sharing
their riches?

Anyway, I swear I'm jinxed when it comes to lotteries
and all those stuff where there's luck involved. It's
frustrating you know.

I've never won anything in my entire life.
I tell you, I think some old gypsy lady must've cursed me
when I was little. Maybe she gave me this huge scar on my
forehead that I just haven't noticed yet. Maybe, just
maybe it is because I'm not meant to have it you know.

Maybe it's that God guy's idea, and I'll just have to live with it. Maybe he's in charge with lotteries and all. About God and all, what a character he is, eh? Putting us through all this horrible life tests and stuff. I just hope heaven is as good as it sounds otherwise all this would have been just so meaningless and all. Gee, it gets overwhelming and I just feel like crying about it sometimes. Hey, I'm a good person I promise. It's … it's just I've been discouraged for so long now, I feel I ought to get all drunk and nasty.

PART THREE

Chapter Twenty One

FRIDAY, LATE IN THE NIGHT

Oh, sorry about that interruption. My mother insisted that we have our evening meal together. Yeah… you guessed it; reason is that it's my birthday and according to my mother people are not supposed to spend birthdays in their room all by themselves.

All that 21st century crap.

Another reason is that my mother's boyfriend, that Michael K., he's gone off somewhere and my mother demanded some company because she and the guy had a good old fight. So Alvy had to show her the sensitive side of who he is, listen to all her relationship/weather talk, and share his 21st birthday. Personally, I don't get it with birthdays.

I mean, really.

Anyway, the meal was good and I must admit I was rather hungry considering all the things I had to get out in the open. I had a few snacks in between, but not nearly enough to satisfy a stylish and good-looking character, who by now must be 'yours truly handsome' or some other fancy phrase that I'm not familiar with. But I think the chocolate cake after supper really did the trick if you'd

ask me. Yeah, I'm quite surprised at the chocolate cake
myself, I really am you know. I could swear the CLEMENS
household is celebrating Christmas or something because it
was probably one of the best chocolate cakes I've ever had
in my entire life! All right so it wasn't the best, but
don't get me wrong, it was a pretty delicious cake that
one and I had a good time eating it.

Whilst eating in the kitchen, my mother, very cheerful
being it my birthday and all, started asking me questions.

'Hmm… hot today wasn't it Alvy?'

'Sure,' I said.

'Because… because this morning it was quite cool. You
remember Alvy?'

'Yup.'

'Well… well I guess Cape Town weather is as
unpredictable as the deep blue sea.'

'Yup,' she said. 'Cape Town weather is as
unpredictable as the deep blue sea.'

'The deep blue sea? How's that?'

'Oh yes, Alvy CLEMENS. The deep blue sea is one place
man knows very little about.'

I'm still wondering how my mother's brain is wired up.
I really do.

'I guess.'

'So how was your day?' she asked.

'Terrific.'

'What you're doing in you're room all the time Alvy CLEMENS? It's your birthday. You know that, don't you?'

'Not much,' I said.

'Are you depressed? Medication is a wonderful thing.'

I looked up and my mother smiled at me. Her teeth looked all old and yellow. Damn cigarettes.

'Just look at me Alvy. Lithium saved my life you know.'

God, I just wanted to eat, get the birthday celebration over with, go back to my room, and kill myself. But that's my mother for you.

'I thought you hated medication. You said Michael K. is medication.' My mother didn't say anything at first. Only later…

'Talk to me, Alvy CLEMENS. It's your birthday. What's wrong?'

I stammered at first. My mother can get quite disturbing sometimes.

'I'm… I'm not, you know… depressed. Gee. Just working on some personal stuff.'

'What kind of stuff?' she asked, 'it's your birthday. You should be out having a good time.'

'Gee relax. Just busy with some stuff.'

'Alvy CLEMENS!'

'Christ, I'm reading this book. It's a… a book on psychology. Very big subject nowadays. Very big. Mom wouldn't understand.'

'Oh, I see. You reading some intellectual stuff?' she asked.

'That's right, I'm going to be famous remember, remember, eh? So I'd better get used to how it'll feel being famous and all by trying to get a understanding of how my mind works, to deal with all the pressures that comes with it. Otherwise I'll end up like that Kennedy. Very challenging if you really want to know.'

'Very interesting,' she said, 'sounds very intellectual to me.'

'Oh it's intellectual. Didn't I say I always wanted to do something intellectual with my life, eh?'

'But Kennedy?' she said. 'I don't understand. What has Kennedy go to do with it?'

'Everything… everything mom. Kennedy never knew of what was coming that day. Poor guy. Never… never even had a suspicion. That's why one has to understand the workings of psychology mom, to… to predict this stuff and prevent this stuff from happening.'

My mom didn't reply. Instead she looked sullen, like a prostitute.

'I remember your father had an interest in psychology,' she eventually said. 'Your father was a man of many talents Alvy. A man of character.'

I wanted to ask her, 'my biological father, the mute, that one?' But I kept my mouth shut.

'Well, Alvy. Happy birthday again. Happy 21st birthday.'

'Thanks mom,' I said.

'Enjoy your psychology stuff after you've finished. If that's what makes you happy.'

'It does.'

I quickly excused myself.

'Oh mom?'

'Yeah.'

'I think I'm going to shoot some rats later on. You know?'

My mother yelled for no reason, 'You and your darn rats!' Gee, I figure that's the bipolar speaking.

'But mom, promise you won't stay up all night for me, O.K.?'

Now that I meant although… if there's an institution in this country that gives courses in how to lie and do it well, I'll send in an application.

Chapter Twenty Two

I'm probably boring you to death right now, eh? I was

half expecting it from this story. Most of the time I
just keep my mouth shut and pretend everything is peaches
and creams in this crazy country of ours and then
suddenly… suddenly I think it's worth telling. It's
ridiculous, all of it, so don't take everything I say too
personally. Seriously I mean it. And please, don't feel
obligated in feeling sorry for me. Just don't.

   Another thing, you may've think by now that I'm very
depressing to be around with because I don't say anything
good about anything or to anyone and… and that I'm
probably the real Yahoo around here, but I promise you I'm
not one of those people. Once you get to know me I swear
you'll like me.

   It's just that sometimes when I go outside and… and I
look around of what's happening here, I get angry because
I don't like what I see and now… now that today is my
birthday and everything, I'm deliberately making it all
sounding worse to you than it actually is because I'm a
little depressed spending my birthday alone.

Well, I guess I have to go now. I've been telling this
meaningless story for the whole damn day and it's driving
me nuts. It really is. I mean, it's not even a story.
Not in a million years. Besides, it's my 21st birthday

and I figure I'm going to celebrate it after all. Yup, I
even got plans to assassinate the President later on
tonight. Nah, just kidding. But who knows, maybe I'll
get a smile on my face before midnight.

Before I go, you probably want to know what my
Christian name is, where I went to school, where I was
born and what my neighbors are like, all that stuff. You
know what? I don't think it's a very good idea. It's too
much of a sensitive subject and besides, I don't want to
scare all my family and friends away because after the
things I shared with you, they… they might never want to
see me ever again. So I guess it's not worth telling you
all that. It's a little too… too out there.

But if there's one thing, just one more thing that I'd
like you to do then it's to forget about everything I said
as quickly as you can because it's just not worth it.

Forget about how I starred in a lousy TV commercial, or
how I wanted to be a stockbroker, or of how I shook hands
with the damn President. It's not such big a deal at the
end of the day trust me.

So I met the President. It didn't change my life, did
it?

Forget about that Koransky girl I fell in love with.

Forget about that depressing Hemingway nutcase.

Forget about Uncle Lennie that died.

Forget about Ronnie and Joe, those irritating intellectuals.

Forget about all the bad things I said to you about my mother because she's actually a very nice middle-aged woman.

Forget about my good looks, forget about my bipolar, and just forget about everyone and everything I told you about because it gets too depressing after a while. It really does.

But most of all, forget about what I said about this crazy place we live in. It's not such a bad place and I actually don't mind living here despite of everything I just told you about.

De Hoop

P.O.B. 10

Riebeek-Kasteel

7307

South Africa

073 795 2701

bruwerh@yahoo.com

The Real Yahoo.

By Hendrik Bruwer

The Real Yahoo.

By Hendrik Bruwer